GLOSSARY

Text Version	Pages 3 – 19
Day 1	Pages 20 – 36
Day 2	Pages 37 – 65
Day 3	Pages 66 – 90
Day 4	Pages 91 – 120
Day 5	Pages 121 – 150
Recovery Plan – 1 Year	Pages 151 – 180
Recovery Plan – 3 Year	Pages 181 – 209
Recovery Plan – 10 Year	Pages 210 – 238
Extra Facilitator Info + How to Become a Facilitator + Authors Note	Pages 239 - 245

Welcome to Radical Recovery Peer Support!

If you are reading this, you may be interested in or have been invited to participate in a Radical Recovery Peer Support group. Therefore, it is worth mentioning that the driving factor of the group is robust participation. We believe that participation increases engagement and reduces the monotony of only having the group Facilitator present material.

All participation in the group is voluntary, however in some instances a person may be mandated to participate. Even in this scenario, the person has the ability to refuse participation which may result in some other option or consequence for them. This is based on their situation and has nothing to do with the group process. Because participation is voluntary, we cannot be sure from one group to another how many people will participate, causing differences from group to group of how much material any one person will present.

Our program offers a certificate of participation and a certificate of completion. People may need a certificate to receive some benefit or to avert a consequence. To receive either certificate, a person will have different participation requirements. Only a certificate of completion will allow a participant to take the next step of becoming a group Facilitator.

Group Facilitators must be able to highly identify with the program. This means that for all the questions other than the ones labeled "how does this passage connect to...," the Facilitator must be able to answer 85% of the questions. Everyone can participate by taking turns reading the material and answering "how does this passage connect to...," but those who are unable to complete at least 85% of the questions may struggle to answer them in group which is why only those seeking a certificate of completion to become Facilitators will answer the questions during group.

While many people may participate in the group for different reasons, we encourage everyone to participate as if they are trying to earn a certificate of completion because it will make the group more dynamic and Peer Supported. The biggest hurdle is determining if you believe you can answer 85% of the questions. Hopefully you will receive a question list or the book a couple weeks before group begins. If that fails, there is at least a week or two between the first group session where no questions are answered, and the second session. We suggest using that time to look over the questions and determine if you can answer 85% of the questions. To earn a certificate of completion your books answers must be checked for quality and completeness.

About This Program:

Radical Recovery Peer Support is a program that utilizes Peer Support to help individuals achieve wellness and personal growth. The author of the program uses first-person inspirational passages to draw parallels between concepts and recovery. The Program Involves group sessions that can be done either in-person or online.

For the group programs, we have three options. This book/group is a group with a focus on higher or continued education called "RRPS-University." RRPS-University emphasizes a crucial element of recovery is getting involved in and taking education serious as a means of achieving a better quality of life. Another version is a general wellness and personal growth group which is simply called Radical Recovery Peer Support. Finally, there is a version of RRPS for Criminal-reentry called "RRPS-Liberation," which discusses developing new belief systems that will help turn our lives around after an arrest.

Over the course of five sessions each group covers important concepts like the Linear Growth Model and Parallel Recovery Concepts. It Also Focuses on the nine Recovery Fundamentals which include principles like Honesty, Trust, Acceptance, Hope, Personal Responsibility, Self-Advocacy, and others. How each group presents the concepts and fundamentals is unique.

The Linear Growth Model recognizes that while growth and recovery are not always linear, putting in effort does often lead to progress over time. Growth may appear uneven, with periods of progress and periods of struggle. However, making consistent efforts through programs like Radical Recovery Peer Support can help us move closer to our hope of achieving stability and wellness.

RRPS is a Cognitive Behavioral Therapy. It is such because the description of the Concepts and Fundamentals, as well as the person first descriptions of the recovery journey address beliefs, thoughts, and feelings commonly experienced in a specific but large audience. Each program addresses thoughts, beliefs, and feelings that held the author back and provides a solution of improving our thoughts, beliefs, and control over our feelings by getting more aligned with positive expressions of Recovery Concepts and Fundamentals.

Examples of how this is done in RRPS - Liberation include changing thoughts for people with criminal history's such as "Only my failures matter," to "I have hope even though its tougher with a record." Changing thoughts of "All probation officers are out to get me" to many of them want to help." Reduces Dichotomous thinking by encouraging the view that its not all black or white or one or the other, but that there are levels of growth on a continuum and a new start can be made at any time.

The programs also incorporate themes of Rational Emotive Therapy in the different events emphasized in each program. With more general distressing circumstances in the original RRPS, to more specific events such as educational neglect in RRPS -University, and the stigma of having a criminal record in RRPS -Liberation, to our beliefs about these issues, and the consequences for results of those beliefs. The program also employs themes of Reality Therapy in its emphasis on personal choice and personal responsibility.

The program also utilizes a wide variety of homework questions that are done outside of group (common of CBT programs) which reinforce the goals of the program. Each Passage that relates an experience based on a Concept or Fundamental usually focuses on a change in thinking that improves each outcome.

Schedule

Session one covers: an introduction to the Linear Growth Model, the Parallel Recovery Concepts, and the 9 Recovery Fundamentals.

Session two Covers: the three Parallel Recovery Concepts.

Session three covers: the first three fundamentals of Honesty, Trust, And Acceptance.

Session four covers: Hope, Personal Responsibility, and Self Advocacy.

Session five covers: Support, Purpose, and Self -actualization.

Goals

This curriculum emphasizes balanced linear growth through development of 9 Recovery Fundamentals and 3 Parallel Recovery Concepts that occur alongside each of the 9 Fundamentals. The goals of this program are based on the Fundamentals of Recovery and the Recovery Concepts and are to teach participants how to:

1. Learn the importance of and how to perform Self-Care
2. Learn to develop a Recovery Plan to take recovery to greater heights (Recovery Planning)
3. learn that while participating in recovery we are at every moment a mentor and a model of recovery behavior
4. overcome challenges, handle stressful or difficult situations and/or troubling thoughts, achieve personal growth and wellness, and live a self-directed life

Goals One, Two, and Three, represent the three Parallel Recovery Concepts of Self-Care, Recovery Planning, and Mentoring - Respectively. Goal four represents the result of successfully incorporating the 9 Recovery Fundamentals into daily life in addition to the Recovery Concepts. On a graph it looks like:

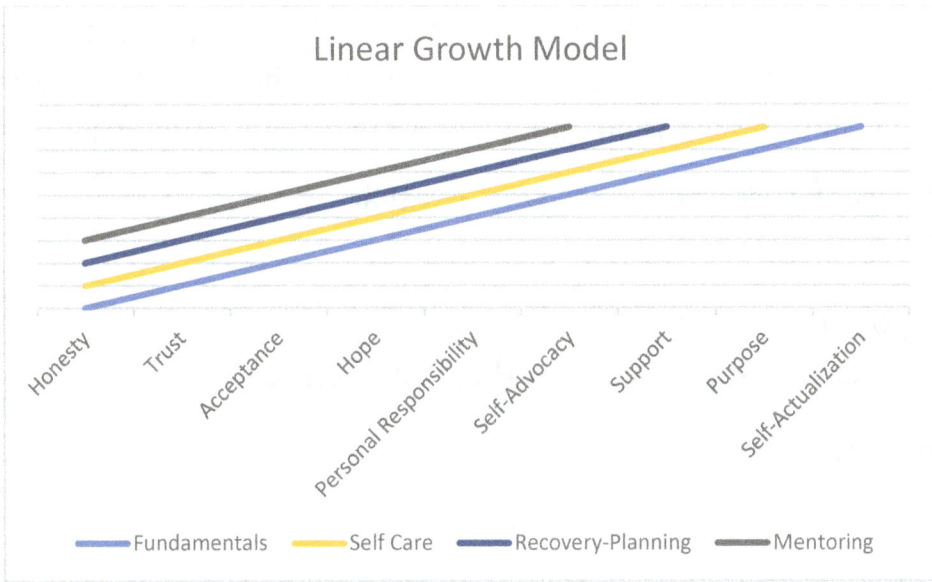

*Tip: Notice that the graph begins with linear growth along the line representing the Fundamentals of Recovery. By implementing the 3 Parallel Recovery Concepts of Self-Care, Recovery Planning, and Mentoring, outcomes and the growth line can be continuously shifted upward to higher levels of growth.

Not only does this program emphasize that every step we take along the path to personal growth and freedom is a moment that encourages others in our society, but it points out that growth is actually fuller and more complete when we remember to care for ourselves, plan for recovery, and when we help others like us, we see that recovery is possible.

From the Better Days workbook passage *'Creating Change':* "Mahatma Gandhi, the great Indian spiritual leader, said, 'Be the change you want to see in the world.' Gregorio Lewis, Author of Better Days Restates this point saying "I say that first I must change myself into the person I want to be."

The words from the passage *'Creating Change'* and Mahatma Gandhi indicate that by learning to focus on our personal experience of growth and change, the world will change in our direction, as we model the behaviors we want to see in the world.

Many programs say that **giving back** and **helping others** with the same problems as we have experienced is a sort of final step. The reasoning behind this program and in Peer Support in general is that showing recovery is possible occurs alongside every stage in the process and our actions create a lasting impact.

In addition, many people who have been successful in recovery say that

- giving back
- taking commitments to support others, and
- remembering that they are an example of recovery in their communities

helped them the most in their recovery.

The 9 Fundamentals of Recovery

Recovery Fundamentals are a set of characteristics that we can use to gauge the strength of our recovery and include but are not limited to:

1. Honesty
2. Trust
3. Acceptance
4. Hope
5. Personal Responsibility
6. Self-Advocacy
7. Support
8. Purpose
9. Self-Actualization

A breakdown of the fundamentals listed first can cause difficulty with fundamentals listed last. The Fundamentals of Recovery are qualities we want to encourage in participants of this program. It is important to remember the quote from Mahatma Ghandi that we should "be the change we want to see in the world." Because we are always Mentors, it is vitally important that we demonstrate the Recovery Fundamentals because our effort, or lack of effort will impact others.

The Linear Growth Model

Growth often does not occur linearly, although many of us wish it did.

What it Usually Looks Like

Our Hopes

What it Could Look Like

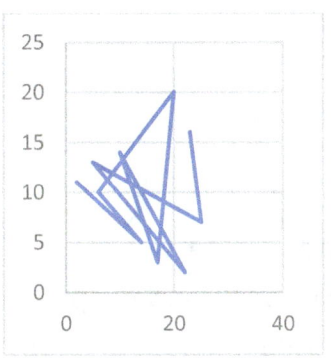
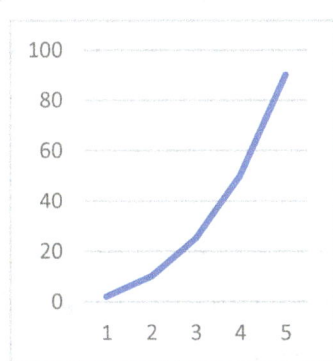
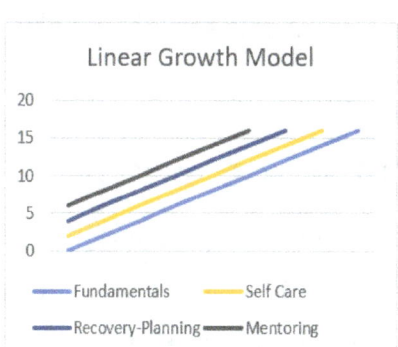

Many recovery programs emphasize that growth is non-linear. However Radical Recovery Peer Support believes that over-emphasizing the non-linear nature of growth is self-defeating. While we acknowledge growth is non-linear, we also believe that in most cases, we do make progress when we put in effort. To over emphasize the non-linear nature of growth tends to give people an excuse to use, such as that there is no guarantee that if they work hard they will grow.

With all the twists and turns and ups and downs of recovery, it can be hard to even tell if growth is occurring. By putting the same amount of effort and care into each of the Recovery Fundamentals, we will get more consistent results than if we were to put all our efforts in one Fundamental.

Because our own actions and behaviors change and impact the world around us, it is common that when we start exhibiting a better relationship with the Recovery Fundamentals, we will experience a mirror effect from the world. We may sometimes wonder why it seems we receive exaggerated reactions or displays of the Fundamentals directed back at us from society but can understand that this may be connected to our own inconsistent demonstrations of the Fundamentals.

The Linear Growth Model gets its name from the idea that

1. Growth is usually Non-Linear

2. we want to put consistent effort into each of the 9 Fundamentals which will result in more, but not all, consistent experiences in our lives.

3. When developed inconsistently with this format, inconsistent and unexpected outcomes may occur.

4. When developed in the order listed previously, each of the 9 Recovery Fundamentals assists in the cultivation and growth of the other Fundamentals.

5. When Utilizing the Parallel Recovery Concepts in conjunction with the Recovery Fundamentals, we can shift our results to a better outcome

False Sense of Security:

When we experience success at Recovery Concepts or the later Fundamentals, particularly starting with Personal Responsibility through Self-Advocacy, Support, and Purpose, we may be lulled into a false sense of security that we are doing well despite shortfalls related to the earlier Fundamentals.

We encourage that no matter our level of success with later Fundamentals, we take a look at how the earlier fundamentals show up for us. Gaps in our development may lead to blind spots that may damage our recovery.

Why We Present the Fundamentals of Recovery and the 3 Parallel Recovery Concepts in This Order

Even though Parallel Recovery Concepts occur throughout our Recovery, there are many reasons for each component that if we do not take proper care of each Recovery Fundamental and Parallel Recovery Concept, we will not unlock the full growth potential of incorporating Recovery Concepts or later Fundamentals into our lives.

We give examples of how neglecting components of the Recovery Concepts and Fundamentals of Recovery leads to a breakdown of the transition to the other components:

Recovery Concepts: This group process and other methods of Recovery can be really hard on us emotionally, mentally, and physically; therefore, it is important that we are kind to ourselves and benefit from this process. From the very beginning of an attempt to better ourselves, such as participating in this group, it will be important to maintain the Recovery Concepts of Self-Care, Recovery Planning, and Mentorship. Right from the beginning it is important to:

- Have a self-care plan, acknowledge the difficulty of this process, and create positive experiences to look forward to
- develop a Recovery plan involving the desired outcome and benefit of this process,
- and recognize that our participation in this process can either help or hinder the recovery of other participants.

Honesty: if we are in fear of what someone will find out about our secrets, harm done to others, past crimes and the things that make us feel guilt, shame, or fear of persecution, we will not know what we can <u>trust</u> others with.

Trust: If we cannot trust ourselves or are not aware of who we can Trust or what systems are working for us and not against us, we will have a hard time finding <u>acceptance</u> of our situation.

Acceptance: If we can't accept our current situation or past experiences and are constantly suffering from them or if someone or some force has an uncomfortable level of control over our lives, we will have a hard time recognizing things we can <u>hope</u> for.

Hope: If we don't have hope and are not propelled by our desire to achieve a hoped-for outcome, the natural inclination is to be unmotivated about our personal responsibilities. If we can't get satisfaction by working on our hopes, we often fail to develop and perform personal responsibilities.

Personal Responsibilities: if we are lacking in fulfilling our personal responsibilities, we often face resistance from others when we self-advocate for ourselves because we have less basis to show that we are capable.

Self-Advocacy: If we fail to effectively advocate for ourselves through means of showing that our capabilities or progress make us a good fit for certain endeavors, or if we advocate for ourselves for that which provides outcomes inconsistent with our recovery, or if we advocate to the wrong people, among other things, we may not get adequate support.

Support: A Significant outcome of working through the Fundamentals of Recovery leading up to support, is that we find ourselves in the best position to begin offering support.

It takes support to fulfil BIG goals. If we do not look for support or accept support from the right people, we will have a hard time achieving our goals. With the added effort it takes to achieve goals without support we have a hard time finding our purpose because everything feels like it is a struggle. Often, things that seem more natural or easier for us, or areas we get the most support, are also area's excellent to find purpose.

Purpose: Without a purpose with which to gauge our progress or put our efforts, we often feel like we are repeating a pattern that rarely changes, or that there is no perceivable pattern but rather instability or lack of focus. Finding and incorporating a purpose into our lives leads to self-actualization, a feeling that we are fulfilling our unique potential

Self-Actualization: This Fundamental of Recovery is often considered a final stage of development. However, to maintain this stage we must continue to put sufficient and equal amounts of effort into all the Fundamentals of Recovery. Also, the Parallel Recovery Concepts must be maintained.

What Mentors Need to Know

Self-Care:

Self-care is any healthy & direct action we take to feel better. Sometimes we need to use Self-Care to respond to stressors, or triggering events, or when we feel like we are in crises. Self-Care that might work normally may not work as well under very difficult conditions.

*Tip for dealing with stressors: One suggestion for how to deal with especially difficult situations is to put more time and effort into the things we usually do to make us feel better.

Really good Self-Care is often planned. Planning Self-Care before we feel unwell has benefits such as having something to look forward to, or helping us not forget Self-Care. Because of this, it is often included in recovery planning.

Examples of Self-Care

- *Remembering our boundaries and what we will or will not do*
- *Spending time with family and friends*
- *Getting enough sleep*
- *Being of service to others*
- *Writing a gratitude list*
- *Taking breaks*

Stressors, burnout, vicarious trauma, poor time management, and compassion fatigue are common reasons we provide Self-Care for ourselves.

Recovery Planning:

Recovery planning is self-determined but often includes friends and family, supporters, or community leaders. Recovery planning is done with the collaboration of individuals involved and utilizes recovery capital.

A Recovery Plan

- *Is based on self-determination*
- *Identifies strengths of the individual and takes inventory of Recovery Capital*
- *Identifies goals, challenges, action steps, and date of completion*
- *May involve support from others and connection to community resources and leadership.*

In a table it looks like:

Goal	Strengths & Recovery Capital	Obstacles	Action Steps	Date of Completion
Get Masters Degree	<ul><li>Have a: bachelors degree</li><li>Time: Am on Disability and am self employed</li><li>Experienced with: online courses</li></ul>	Classes are condensed so more is required in a shorter time.	<ul><li>Clear agenda for first week</li><li>Start each day with school first</li><li>Complete all assignments before recreation</li></ul>	August 10th 2025

Recovery plans need to be evaluated and measured for progress. Criteria for evaluation should come from the person creating the plan and should be considered before action, if possible.

Mentoring:

Mentoring is a constant ongoing process and occurs in situations where we present both the best or worst aspects of ourselves. We never know just what kind of impact we will have on others. Remember the words of Mahatma Gandhi – "be the change you want to see in the world." One way to effect change is through Mentoring.

- Mentoring provides an opportunity to be there for a person in a way that supports them in both the best of times and the worst
- A good mentor will respect each person's unique approach to recovery
- A Mentor utilizes self-disclosure in a way that does not compete with but rather informs an individual of shared experiences
- A Mentor should be primarily focused on the person they are mentoring; only sharing about themselves or their experiences when it would be a benefit to the mentee
- Mentoring is constant and ongoing, and occurs in situations where we present both the best or worst aspects of ourselves
- We never know just what kind of impact we will have on others

Honesty:

Many of us have Baggage. In recovery, we may resist new healthy behaviors and thoughts. This may often stem from a lack of honesty about three factors, 1: that we have been hurt and/or 2: that we have hurt ourselves or others, and 3: the nature of the severity of the hurt.

It is important to acknowledge

- if we are not honest within ourselves about how we have been hurt, hurt ourselves or others, or the severity, we may repeat unfavorable experiences.

Trust:

There are different levels of trust - We can have trust in:

- a specific person or people that we trust
- in the systems we are in such as our governments, legal system, or system of wellness or therapy
- self-trust; <u>trusting that we have our own best interests in mind</u>.

Within these is determining who we can rely on, who we cannot, and what we can share with others.

*Tip – Self-disclosure: It is important to remember

- we never need to share something that would make us uncomfortable
- there is more we can share with others than something that would make us uncomfortable
- it is different to share things we want to keep private versus our hopes, goals, and stresses
- there is no guarantee what we say will remain confidential

Acceptance:

Each person is subject to different degrees of unforeseen circumstances, restrictions, rules, and regulations. For the most part, these obstacles depend on our situation, can be temporary, or can be changed with support. While we must deal with these situations while they occur, we can find ways to have hope within them and have Better Days.

*Tip – Trauma/Grief Informed: Many people will report that there are things that they cannot or will not accept. This is okay, remind them that they can still work on other Fundamentals and that there is a difference between 1: accepting that an event took place and 2: accepting an event into our lives and our space.

Hope:

If we are struggling to find hope, it will often become easier the longer we commit to recovery and through more time between distressing events. Also, <u>actively seek out inspiration</u> by:

- talking to supporters about what is giving our supporters hope
- making lists of things that give us hope
- reading recovery stories
- list their own dreams, and if possible, communicate them to someone

Personal Responsibility:

Some situations may be out of our control or cause discomfort for us. If we are having a hard time fulfilling responsibilities because of obstacles, things outside our control, or things we need or are worried about; we can ask how much control we have over these situations, and if we are doing everything we can within the control we have.

Personal Responsibility Continued -

To get back on track we can follow a Recovery Plan that involves:

- A daily plan
- A plan of things we need to do every now and then
- A plan for achieving big goals

Plans should include a way to provide for ourselves and elements of Self-Care

If we are developing a Recovery Plan, it is important to first list things we struggle with, things that need the most attention, or that create new responsibilities for us. A Recovery Plan is a way to familiarize ourselves with our objectives and requirements and decide how things need to be done.

Personal Responsibility may involve creating goals that improve our lives and our success. For information on how to help someone with their goals, refer to the section of the RRPS Mentors Guide titled Motivational Interviewing & Recovery Planning.

Self-Advocacy:

Sometimes people may feel they have lost their right or ability to advocate for themselves, or that they have lost control of their lives. Each person has the right to advocate for themselves for the same public benefits and treatment common to their society no matter what the state of their lives.

*Tip – if a person is having a hard time gaining support through self-advocacy, communicate that

- our chances of getting support increase the longer we maintain continued effort with the Recovery Fundamentals that precede this step, especially Personal Responsibility.

- we can believe in ourselves and practice advocating by making a list of goals we think will get the most support and advocating for each item on the list.

Support:

"It takes support to fulfill BIG goals. If we do not look for support or accept support from the right people, we will have a tougher time achieving our goals."

If we lack support, developing a strong support system benefits from:

- being mutually supportive to others
- doing everything within our control to maintain our personal definition of wellness
- becoming active in the community, a support group, school, or other area like employment
- having several supporters so someone will always be available, and we do not overburden anyone

Purpose:

Once we have maintained progress relevant to our interests and security, are more empowered, and have support, we may find that other people are an extension of ourselves or that we have integrated a cause into our lives.

We may also find that

- human rights,
- dignity, and
- freedom become important to us.

Self-Actualization:

Self-actualization is all about reaching the true potential of our unique selves. Once we have reached our full potential, we may find that we are freer and more capable. Often, people at this level of development begin to have a deeper connection with where they believe they fit in the universe, existence, and in relation to other people or their concept of a higher power.

In the *Allegory of the Cave* "Plato's Republic," the principal character in the story returns to people that were still "disillusioned" to help them find a better way. For most this is a natural inclination by this stage of recovery, to show others a brighter future. The Parallel Recovery Concept of Mentorship has carried many individuals' recoveries to particularly new heights. Consider the shift in the growth demonstrated in the Linear Growth Model due to the Parallel Recovery Concepts and Mentorship.

Presentation Process

The slides that can be read in the workbook or PowerPoint will be divided between all those wishing to receive a certificate of participation or completion, including participation from the facilitators. The Facilitators will start by explaining why we request full participation and the reward of either a certificate of completion or participation. The Information on participation requirements is on page two underneath the table of contents.

The Facilitators will read the first two slides of the first presentation. After that, all slides will be divided up between the participants. The exceptions to this are the slides in the first session's presentation following the slide title "Why We Present the Recovery Fundamentals and Parallel Recovery Concepts in this Order." These slides sometimes contain more than one Fundamental or Concept and there will be a different reader for each of these.

At the end of each session, the Facilitator will read the last slide that conveys information related to the upcoming session. After this, the remainder of the time will be spent on open discussion of the day's session. For session one this will be the full span of 2 hours, for the remaining session it will be the span of 3 hours.

The remaining sessions also have sections titled 'How does this passage connect or relate to the concept or fundamental.' These questions entail a short response that should connect the passage read just before this question to the Recovery Concept or Fundamental being discussed at the time. Everyone has the capability to answer these questions so everyone desiring a certificate of participation or completion will answer these including the facilitator, unless facilitator participation means some participants will not have the chance to participate.

Participation points will not be lost for these questions if there were not enough questions for everyone to get a chance to participate. A participation sheet will be provided which specifies how many participation points a person will need in each category of participation. For those who have not had a chance to answer these questions, they will have an opportunity to revisit them at the end of the group.

Sessions 2 – 5 also have many short questions. There are usually 3 questions for each passage. These are divided between all those seeking a certificate of completion and the Facilitators. These questions are not required to be answered by those seeking a certificate of participation.

The Facilitator will not participate or read unless there are fewer than 5 people attempting a certificate of completion, in which case, only participating when they have the least amount of participation compared to those seeking a certificate. Participants can choose when they would like to participate in order to get the right amount of participation points, however when some of them are close to full points, the facilitator will begin asking specific people to participate if a participant has the least amount of participation.

If participants do not have a response to a particular question, the Facilitator will step in and answer the question. If participants did not get enough participation points from this question-and-answer section, we can allow them to answer other questions from the session at the end as a revisitation.

To revisit a question requires them to have completed enough of their answers to share them and receive the required completion points. This might be useful for participants that did not complete enough of their questions before the group where the questions they did answer in the book were answered by other participants. Even if the participant did not complete a question before group, we can allow them to develop a quick answer on the spot if they are able.

Once the presentation process is over for the session, we allow the rest of the time to be open discussion starting with the facilitator asking the group if they have any questions, allowing participants to ask questions here. Next, we will do a check in, asking the group how they are doing with the concepts or fundamentals covered in the session. Once 2 hours have elapsed for session one, or three hours for all other sessions, the session is complete.

This is how the group will be Facilitated.

P.s.

On the last page of each day's session, the text will also point out what needs to be completed before the next day's session. All assignments discussed on these pages will be shared by participants in breakout rooms if the group is online, or with the person sitting next to them if done in person.

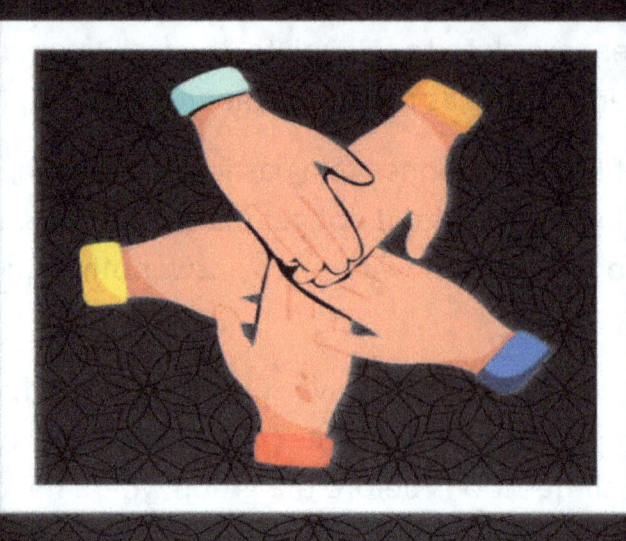

Radical Recovery Peer Support- University

Day 1

This curriculum emphasizes balanced linear growth through the development of 9 Recovery Fundamentals and three Parallel Recovery Concepts that occur alongside each of the 9 Fundamentals.

The goals of this program are based on the Fundamentals of Recovery and the Recovery Concepts. They are:

Learn the importance of and how to perform Self-Care

Learn to develop a Recovery Plan to take recovery to greater heights (Recovery Planning)

Overcome challenges or troubling thoughts, handle stressful or difficult situations, achieve personal growth and wellness, and live a self-directed life

Learn that while participating in recovery we are at every moment a mentor and a model of recovery behavior

From the Better Days workbook passage 'Creating Change': "Mahatma Gandhi, the great Indian spiritual leader, said, 'Be the change you want to see in the world.'

Gregorio Lewis, Author of Better Days restates this point by saying "I say that first I must change myself into the person I want to be."

The words from the passage *'Creating Change'* and Mahatma Gandhi indicate that by learning to focus on our personal experience of growth and change, the world will change in our direction, as we model the behaviors we want to see in the world.

Many programs say that **giving back** and **helping others** with the same problems as we have experienced is a sort of final step. The reasoning of this program and in Peer Support in general is that showing recovery is possible occurs alongside every stage in the process and our actions create a lasting impact.

In addition, many people who have been successful in recovery say that

- giving back
- taking commitments to support others, and
- remembering that they are an example of recovery in their communities

helped them the most in their recovery.

The 9 Recovery Fundamentals

Recovery Fundamentals are a set of characteristics that we can use to gauge the strength of our recovery and include but are not limited to:

- Honesty
- Trust
- Acceptance
- Hope
- Personal Responsibility
- Self-Advocacy
- Support
- Purpose
- Self-Actualization

A breakdown of the Fundamentals listed first can cause difficulty with the Fundamentals listed last

NOTES:

Parallel Recovery Concepts

Self Care

Recovery Planning

Mentoring

Growth often does not occur linearly, although many of us wish it did – Imagine if you knew X amount of effort led to Y amount of growth!

- We often hope growth would look like this

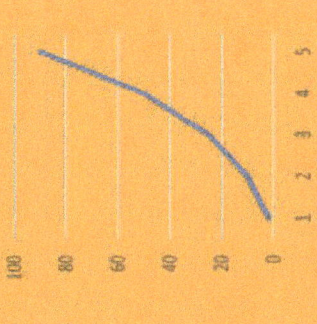

- What it usually looks like

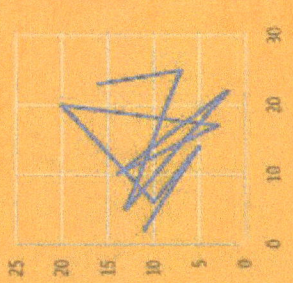

The Linear Growth Model

Growth we can aim for

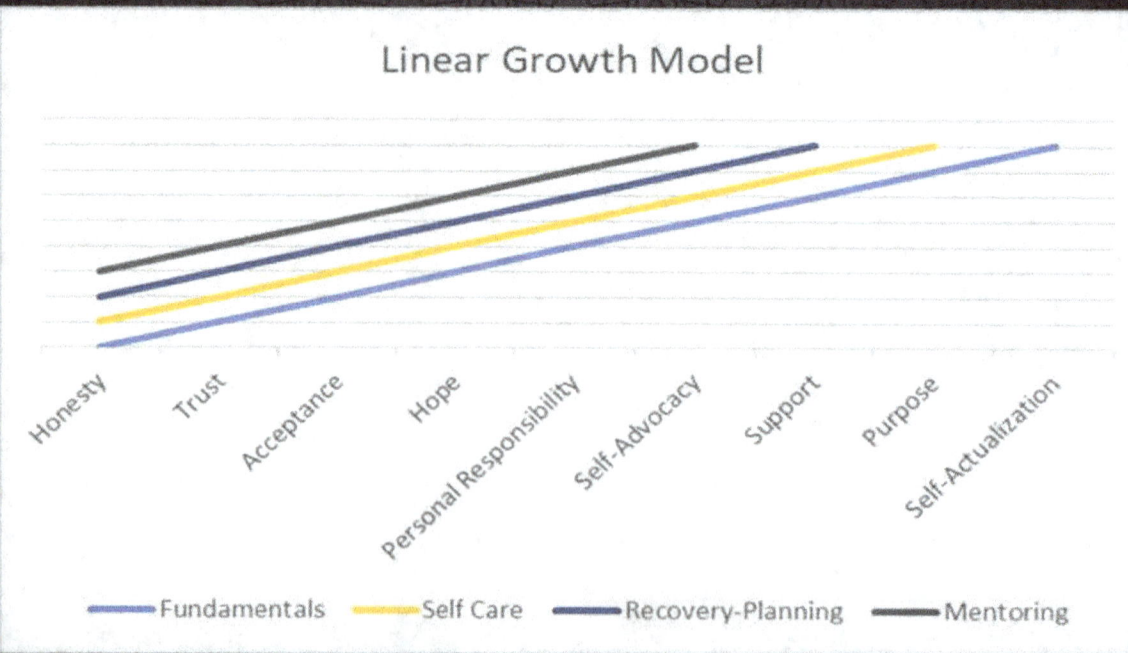

The Linear Growth Model (Continued)

The Linear Growth Model gets its name from the idea that

1. Growth is usually Non-Linear

2. We want to put consistent effort into each of the 9 Fundamentals which will result in more, but not all, consistent experiences in our lives.

3. When developed inconsistently with this format, inconsistent and unexpected outcomes may occur.

4. When developed in the order listed previously, each of the 9 Recovery Fundamentals assists in the cultivation and growth of the other Fundamentals.

5. When Utilizing the Parallel Recovery Concepts in conjunction with the Recovery Fundamentals, we can shift our results to a better outcome

The Linear Growth Model (Continued)

With all the twists and turns and ups and downs of recovery, it can be hard to even tell if growth is occurring. By putting the same amount of effort and care into each of the Recovery Fundamentals, we will get more consistent results than if we were to put all our efforts in one Fundamental.

Because our own actions and behaviors change and impact the world around us, it is common that when we start exhibiting a better relationship with the Recovery Fundamentals, we will experience a mirror effect from the world. We may sometimes wonder why it seems we receive exaggerated reactions or displays of the Fundamentals directed back at us from society but can understand that this may be connected to our own inconsistent demonstrations of the Fundamentals.

False Sense of Security

When we experience success at Recovery Concepts or the later Fundamentals, particularly starting with Personal Responsibility through Self-Advocacy, Support, and Purpose, we may be lulled into a false sense of security that we are doing well despite shortfalls related to the earlier Fundamentals.

We encourage that no matter our level of success with later Fundamentals, we take a look at how the earlier fundamentals show up for us. Gaps in our development may lead to blind spots that may damage our recovery.

Why We Present the Recovery Fundamentals and Parallel Recovery Concepts in This Order

There are many reasons that if we do not take proper care of each Recovery Fundamental and Parallel Recovery Concept, we will not unlock the full growth potential of incorporating Recovery Concepts or Fundamentals into our lives.

We give examples of how neglecting components of the Recovery Concepts and Fundamentals leads to a breakdown of the transition to the other components:

Recovery Concepts:

This group process and other methods of Recovery can be hard on us emotionally, mentally, and physically; therefore, it is important that we are kind to ourselves and benefit from this process.

From the very beginning of an attempt to better ourselves, such as participating in this group, it will be important to maintain the Recovery Concepts of Self-Care, Recovery Planning, and Mentorship.

Right from the beginning it is important to:

- Have a self-care plan, acknowledge the difficulty of this process, and create positive experiences to look forward to

- develop a Recovery plan involving the desired outcome and benefit of this process,

- and recognize that our participation in this process can either help or hinder the recovery of other participants.

Recovery Fundamentals:

Honesty: if we are in fear of what someone will find out about our secrets, harm done to others, past crimes, and the things that make us feel guilt, shame, or fear of persecution, we will not know what we can trust others with.

Trust: If we cannot trust ourselves or are not aware of who we can Trust or what systems are working for us and not against us, we will have a hard time finding acceptance of our situation.

Acceptance: If we can't accept our current situation or past experiences and are constantly suffering from them or if someone or some force has an uncomfortable level of control over our lives, we will have a hard time recognizing things we can hope for.

Recovery Fundamentals:

Hope: If we don't have any hope and are not propelled by our desire to achieve a hoped-for outcome, the natural inclination is to be unmotivated about our personal responsibilities. If we can't get satisfaction by working on our hopes, we often fail to develop and perform personal responsibilities.

Personal Responsibilities: if we are lacking in fulfilling our personal responsibilities, we often face resistance from others when we self-advocate for ourselves because we have less basis to show that we are capable.

Self-Advocacy: If we fail to effectively advocate for ourselves through means of showing that our capabilities or progress make us a good fit for certain endeavors, or if we advocate for ourselves for that which provides outcomes inconsistent with our recovery, or if we advocate to the wrong people, among other things, we may not get adequate support.

Recovery Fundamentals:

<u>Support</u>: A Significant outcome of working through the Recovery Fundamentals leading up to support, is that we find ourselves in the best position to begin offering support.

It takes support to fulfil BIG goals. If we do not look for support or accept support from the right people, we may have a hard time achieving our goals. With the added effort it takes to achieve goals without support, we have a hard time finding our <u>purpose</u> because of the effort and struggle. Often, things that seem more natural or easier for us, or areas where we get the most support, are also the area's excellent to find purpose.

Recovery Fundamentals:

<u>Purpose</u>: Without a purpose with which to gauge our progress or put our efforts, we often feel like we are repeating a pattern that rarely changes, or that there is no perceivable pattern but rather instability or lack of focus. Finding and incorporating a purpose into our lives leads to <u>self-actualization</u>, a feeling that we are fulfilling our unique potential.

<u>Self-Actualization</u>: This Recovery Fundamental is often considered a final stage of development. However, to maintain this stage we must continue to put sufficient and equal amounts of effort into each of the Recovery Fundamentals. Also, a benefit can be found in incorporating the Parallel Recovery Concepts.

Stages of Wellness and Recovery:

Stage one
1- Learning about recovery
2- Exercising choice
3- Seeking services i.e. counseling, therapy, medication, detox, peer support
4 - Staying away from harmful behaviors
5 - Staying away from negative influences, places or people
6 - Ending the pattern of isolation
7 - Finding positive role models
8 - Learning to ask for support
9 - Becoming personally responsible
10 - Experiencing joy and distress that can be overwhelming at times (extreme but fickle)

Stage 2
1 - Increase in physical health
2 - Ability to distinguish between different feelings and handle them
3 - Reducing emotions that interfere with our wellbeing
4 - Changes in thoughts, feelings and beliefs
5 - Zoning in on negative behaviors
6 - Having experienced the benefits of recovery, becoming committed to recovery

Stage 3
1 - Desire to make amends for harm we caused before we began recovery
2 - Becoming the "change we want to see in the world"
3 - Learning not to inflict self-harm or create hardship
4 - Developing honest and trusting relationships with more people

Stage 4
1 - Ability to use our strengths & knowledge to seize opportunities
2 - Automatic use of wellness tools and coping skills
3 - Self-forgiveness
4 - Building loving relationships rather than dependent ones
5 - Experiencing enduring happiness

Stage 5
1 - Becoming Self-actualized
2 - Gaining confidence, gratitude, and acceptance
3 - Developing integrity and humility
4 - Significant reduction of fear

Stage 6 - Celebration & Maintenance

The Guiding Principles of Recovery
Taken from SAMHSA

Hope – belief that recovery is possible. When Hope is internalized and promoted by others, it is a key driver of recovery.

Person-driven – People define their own goals and the path to reaching them.

Many Pathways/Roads – Recovery is highly personalized and different for each person.

Holistic – Recovery emphasizes mind, body, spirit, and community.

Peer Support – Peers encourage and engage each other.

Relational – Recovery is supported by people who believe in a person's ability to recover.

Culture – Traditions, beliefs, and values are important in defining a person's recovery journey and path.

Trauma-informed – Services should promote safety and trust, creating choice, empowerment, and collaboration.

Strengths & Responsibilities – Individuals, communities, and families have strengths and resources that can benefit recovery. Individuals have the responsibility for their own recovery, but family and community support is essential.

Respect – acceptance and appreciation is key to recovery. This includes respect from other people and a respect for ourselves that helps us develop a positive identity and confidence.

What Mentors should know

- Peer Support is **Self-directed** and works on the principle that clients are the experts on their own experiences and needs. It is a type of therapy based on the idea that each person can become more self-aware, take charge of their own lives, and improve. It is **Person-driven** – People define their own goals and the path to reaching them.

- Peer Support uses **Empathy** a key component of emotional intelligence. **Empathy** is the ability to understand and accurately perceive the internal experiences of another person. In client-centered counseling, Supporters try to show empathy by actively listening to clients, considering their feelings and experiences, and communicating and accepting them.

- In Peer Support, **empowerment** can come from facilitating self discovery and growth by allowing people to to make their own choices and decisions based on their own values, priorities, and goals. The therapist supports the client in identifying their strengths, resources, and areas for growth and assists them in developing coping strategies, problem-solving skills, and self-care practices. **Empathy** also helps counteract **learned helplessness** by creating a safe and supportive environment where clients feel **empowered** to take ownership of their lives and make positive changes.

What Mentors should know

- The **Trauma Informed Approach** demands trust and safety at all levels. This practice encourages choice, collaboration, and empowerment. To practice the Trauma informed approach, request and accommodate feedback as to how to increase the safety of the environment, increase trust by practicing genuineness, and create choice by using open ended and permission questions.

- **Stages of Change** – Stages of change include **Precontemplation, Contemplation, Preparation, Action, and Maintenance**. Often mentors will fail helping someone change behaviors because they do not approach change in the order previously listed. In Precontemplation we educate and develop discrepancy, in Contemplation we encourage and view pros and cons, in Preparation we dismantle barriers, in Action we validate, in Maintenance we should encourage consistency and acquiring more skills related to successful outcomes related to the goal or behavior.

- Some **Cognitive Behavioral Therapy (CBT)** is outside the scope of a Peer Recovery Supporter. Various practices like desensitization techniques and use of imagery are concepts best left to qualified clinicians. However, **relaxation therapy** may be utilized as well as **cognitive behavioral workbooks** that are crafted to address **thoughts, beliefs, and feelings** in a way that does not create excessive pressure on the mentee. Person centered techniques such as building trust and rapport are often helpful but not required as some mentees prefer a more distant expert approach, however this too is outside the scope of a Peer Recovery Supporter.

Differentiate between the medical model and the wellness-focused approach to recovery.

The Medical Model is primarily related to Psychiatry. In the medical model, expert Psychiatrists consider the problems being experienced to be related to genetic inheritance or chemical imbalances. They rely on Medication Assisted Therapy to cause positive change in their patients. This is different from the approach of a Social Worker, Therapist, or Peer Supporter.

A Wellness-focused Approach often involves Peer Support, or the support of someone with lived experience of mental health or substance use; moreover, it considers Social Determinants of Health such as housing, employment, and social support as significant factors of wellbeing.

A Wellness-focused Approach involves **growth, meaning, purpose,** and **empowerment** beyond the problem, which helps a person live the life they want to live.

Day 2

Make sure to prepare for the special exercise found in the section for Self-Care.

Self-Care requires us to make a list of 5 wellness activities we can use to help ourselves feel better. We will discuss our lists of wellness activities in group or in breakout rooms. Please be prepared ahead of time.

Please complete responses to passages and questions included in future groups such as "Day 2" before the next group.

Instructions for passage responses – 1) response must include 5 keywords found in the passage itself. 2) Ensure that the keywords get underlined, so we know which ones you used. 3) the Recovery Concept or Fundamental being linked to the passage must be mentioned twice in the response.

NOTES:

Radical Recovery Peer Support – Univesity Day 2

Insights on Self-Care

Self-care is any healthy action we take to feel better. Sometimes we use Self-Care to respond to stressors, triggering events, or when we feel like we are in crisis. Self-Care that might work normally may not work as well under very difficult conditions.

Tip for dealing with stressors: One suggestion for how to deal with especially difficult situations is to put more time and effort into the things we usually do to make us feel better.

Really good Self-Care is often planned. Planning Self-Care before we feel unwell has benefits, such as, having something to look forward to or helping us not forget Self-Care. Because of this, it is often included in recovery planning.

Examples of Self-Care

- Remembering our boundaries and what we will or will not do
- Being of service to others
- Writing a gratitude list
- Spending time with family and friends
- Getting enough sleep
- Taking breaks

Stressors, burnout, vicarious trauma, poor time management, and compassion fatigue are common reasons we provide Self-Care for ourselves.

- The assignment "how does this passage relate to…?" must include 5 keywords from the passage itself which cannot be used or counted more than once. In addition, the Recovery Concept or Fundamental must be mentioned at least twice in the assignment. <u>Words that do not convey a concept like we, the, or, or a, will not be counted.</u>

- Variations of words that are <u>used in the passages</u> are accepted such as changing "Simple" to "Simplest."

- You must underline the keywords you use.

Self-care

In the past, I struggled tremendously with over-committing myself without paying attention to my own needs and limitations. Whether it was taking on too many responsibilities at work without breaks, not getting enough sleep due to cramming for exams, or neglecting basic self-care activities like healthy meals and exercise, when papers and projects piled up, I had a bad habit of running myself into the ground.

I have come to realize through experience that this type of approach ends up backfiring more often than not. When I am stressed, overwhelmed, unhealthy or unbalanced, it becomes so much harder for me to focus clearly on my studies and perform to the best of my abilities.

Taking time for rest, nourishment, leisure activities and stress relief has made a huge difference in my ability to manage my academic workload sustainably over time. Activities like documenting my weekly time usage has helped me identify time draining activities I can reduce or eliminate, allowing me to better focus energy where it's needed.

Example - How Does the Passage connect to Self-Care?

The person sharing the quote had problems with <u>overcommitting</u> and taking on too many <u>responsibilities</u>. They didn't look out for their own <u>needs</u> or <u>limitations</u>. Taking time for <u>rest, nourishment, and leisure activities</u> was a form of self-care that made a huge difference for them.

Performing time management functions like <u>documenting</u> time usage was a form of self-care that helped them better focus their energy.

How Does the Passage connect to Self-Care or Resonate with You?

HOMEWORK

Question - 1:
How does your past approach to academic responsibilities relate to your current views on self-care and burnout prevention.

HOMEWORK

Question - 2:

In what areas of your life do you struggle with overcommitting yourself without paying attention to your own needs and limitations?

HOMEWORK

Question - 3:

In what ways does overcommitting affect your ability to manage responsibilities overtime?

HOMEWORK

Self-care

Self-care can take up some of our time, which we might not have much of, but it actually increases our performance, helps us focus on and finish our work faster, and increases our energy levels. Monitoring my energy levels and knowing when to take breaks has been helpful. When I begin to feel burned out, fatigued or overwhelmed with my academic responsibilities, taking time to do something nice for myself helps recharge my batteries.

Even simple acts of self-care like taking a relaxing shower or bath, reading a fun book, calling a supportive friend or spending time in nature have made a big difference. Doing something just for me to refresh my mind allows me to return to my studies feeling happier and more peaceful.

I also focus on hobbies I find genuinely enjoyable during break times, whether that's listening to music, drawing, or watching YouTube videos about my interests, or other simple pleasures. Staying balanced by incorporating self-care into my recovery plan has helped me support my education better.

How Does the Passage connect to Self-Care or Resonate with You?

HOMEWORK

Question - 1:
What specific self-care activities help you to better manage your workload and prevent burnout?

HOMEWORK

Question - 2:
What are some ways you can identify when you begin to feel burned out, fatigued, or overwhelmed with your academic responsibilities?

HOMEWORK

Question - 3:

What are 3 of the simplest acts of self-care that you can incorporate into your life and how could these activities boost your well-being and motivation as a student?

HOMEWORK

1-

2-

3-

Homework – Provide a List of Wellness Activities

1

2

3

4

5

NOTES:

Recovery Planning

Recovery planning is self-determined but often includes friends and family, supporters, or community leaders. Recovery planning is done with the collaboration of individuals involved and utilizes recovery capital.

A Recovery Plan

- *Is based on self-determination*

- *Identifies strengths of the individual and takes inventory of Recovery Capital*

- *Identifies goals, challenges, action steps, and date of completion*

- *may involve support from others and connection to community resources and leadership.*

- *need to be evaluated and measured for progress. Criteria for evaluation should come from the person creating the plan and should be considered before action, if possible.*

What a Recovery Plan Looks Like on Paper

Goal	Strengths & Recovery Capital	Challenges	Action Steps	Date of Completion
Get Masters Degree	<ul><li>Have a: bachelors degree</li><li>Time: Am on Disability and am self employed</li><li>Experienced with: online courses</li></ul>	Classes are condensed so more is required in a shorter time.	<ul><li>Clear agenda for first week</li><li>Start each day with school first</li><li>Complete all assignments before recreation</li></ul>	August 10th 2025

In the space provided on the extended pages for the recovery Plan, you may also want to include the people who can support you in each goal.

Recovery Planning

For many who pursue recovery, higher education may not have been a priority during their youth because of undue influences or a lack of proper role models. Recovery involves regaining what was lost, and for some education was lost or deprioritized at a young age.

Recovery planning can help people set education and career related goals that promote self-actualization which is an important part of recovery and living a self-directed life. Pursuing higher education through recovery planning provides an opportunity to return to a prior status or path in life before various influences may have led us off course.

Planning for things like seeking support through community involvement, mentorship, and peer support can aid recovery during higher education by promoting well-being, positive identity, and avoiding the kind of isolation that could lead back to old behaviors. The support available in colleges, such as advising, tutoring, study groups and financial aid benefited my recovery directly and helped me succeed academically and develop in my career. This is why for me, I made education part of my recovery plan.

How Does the Passage connect to Recovery Planning or Resonate with You?

HOMEWORK

Question - 1:

Was higher education ever part of your plan growing up? Describe one thing that either held you back in school or helped you in your education growing up.

HOMEWORK

Question - 2:

How could developing education and career related goals as part of a recovery plan help regain what was lost or deprioritized in your life?

HOMEWORK

Question - 3:

What are some ways that seeking out a qualified mentor or supporter to help you create your recovery plan could promote wellbeing and positive identity while pursuing your career goals?

HOMEWORK

Recovery Planning

Struggling is a natural part of the recovery process. For those in recovery pursuing higher education, struggling can take on additional forms, such as juggling academic responsibilities with personal life challenges like mental health, legal issues, or work and family life. However, with acceptance of our circumstances and a commitment to persistent effort, we can use struggles as opportunities to refine our resilience.

Learning better ways to manage tough times is key to feeling happier and healthier long term for those continuing their education. That's why it is good to have a recovery plan that accounts for the specifics of what we need to accomplish.

By planning my recovery process through perspectives like these, I felt more in control during tough periods and better equipped to succeed academically. When I was struggling, I gained the power to help myself move forward, and with a committed effort to my recovery plan I will achieve my goal. For me, higher education is a valid part of the recovery plan that supports feeling better by enabling me to improve my ability to create change in my life.

How Does the Passage connect to Recovery Planning or Resonate with You?

HOMEWORK

Question - 1:

What are some specific life challenges that someone pursuing their education while also pursuing Wellness and recovery may struggle with alongside juggling academic responsibilities?

HOMEWORK

Question - 2:

Why could having a plan that accounts for the specifics of what you need to accomplish help you gain a sense of control during hardship.

HOMEWORK

Question - 3:

What are some key short-term goals that would help you feel better equipped to succeed academically?

HOMEWORK

NOTES:

MENTORING

- Mentoring provides an opportunity to be there for a person in a way that supports them in both the best of times and the worst

- A Mentor utilizes self-disclosure in a way that does not compete with but rather informs an individual of shared experiences

- A good mentor will respect each person's unique approach to recovery

- A Mentor should be primarily focused on the person they are mentoring; only sharing about themselves when it would benefit the mentee

- We never know just what kind of impact we will have on others

- Mentoring is constant and ongoing, and occurs in situations where we present the best or worst aspects of ourselves

What Mentors Should Do

- Participate as a member of the individual's treatment team.
- Guarantee that recovery is based on the individual's strengths and resiliencies.
- Support the individual in defining spirituality on their own terms.
- Assist others to develop problem-solving skills.
- Assure that relationships, services and supports, reflect individual differences and cultural diversity.
- Support the individual's use of self-determination.
- Model acceptance and cultural humility.
- Partner with individuals to assist them in identifying their strengths, challenges to recovery and recovery capital.
- Apply Motivational Interviewing to assist individuals in during stages of change.
- Inform individuals of their options related to decisions that affect their recovery.

What Mentors Should Do

- Identify personal issues that negatively impact one's ability to perform mentor duties and perform appropriate self care before assisting others further.
- Utilize consultation regarding dual relationships.
- Utilize de-escalation techniques and educate individuals on suicide prevention concepts.
- Partner with the individual to access recovery-oriented services and supports
- Support the individual to identify options and participate in decisions connected to creating and completing recovery goals.
- Promote a wellness-focused approach to recovery.
- Utilize supervision and consultation regarding harm to self and others.
- Respond appropriately to personal stressors, triggers and indicators.
- Utilize trauma-informed care approaches.
- Assess the mentee's satisfaction with his/her progress toward recovery goals.

Mahatma Gandhi

- Remember the words of Mahatma Gandhi – **"be the change you want to see in the world."**
- One way to effect change is through Mentoring.

Mentoring

When I first started thinking about continuing my education after some past challenges, I felt overwhelmed by both academics and responsibilities outside of school. However, connecting with a Mentor who genuinely supported my well-being and success made a world of difference.

Through regular meetings with my Mentor, I was able to work through issues that had long held me back from achievement. They helped me establish meaningful life goals for the first time and navigate difficulties like legal matters. My Mentor also suggested productive groups and activities that aided my recovery by preventing isolation. Connecting to others in the community through these supports was important for my engagement in recovery and academics.

Additionally, my Mentor boosted my confidence to believe in my potential and form real goals. Their guidance helped me imagine higher accomplishments for myself.

How Does the Passage connect to Mentoring or Resonate with You?

HOMEWORK

Question– 1:
What are some issues that previously held you back from achievement that a mentor could help you work through?

HOMEWORK

Question– 2:
How could connecting with a mentor who supports your well-being and success aid recovery from past challenges?

HOMEWORK

Question– 3:
How could being a mentor for others with similar experiences who are looking to pursue higher education provide benefits to you or another person. Would being a mentor help you feel fulfilled?

HOMEWORK

Mentoring

When I began to truly feel like I could succeed at this school stuff and began to understand the industry in which I was learning about, I began to believe I could succeed and felt compelled to help others gain the same feeling. I didn't have all the answers and wasn't the best of all the other students, but I began mentoring others who were truly struggling and discovered some new personal strengths in the process.

Seeking to give back, I connected with fellow students on social media. In meeting many other dedicated students, I found the best and most motivated among them who truly wanted guidance. Mentoring these individuals to support their success helped me develop confidence and relationships that benefited my career goals.

By accepting my role and responsibilities as a mentor, I practice important recovery fundamentals daily. Our meetings require demonstrating honesty, trust, acceptance, and personal accountability without any judgment. In turn, mentoring others reinforces these values and concepts in my own education and Wellness.

How Does the Passage connect to Mentoring or Resonate with You?

HOMEWORK

Question– 1:

What personal strengths do you feel you have that could help you help another person? How could using these strengths as a mentor help you further develop your confidence and career goals?

HOMEWORK

Question– 2:

Mentoring requires demonstrating honesty, trust, acceptance, and personal accountability. Which of these characteristics do you feel you are the strongest in and why?

HOMEWORK

Question– 3:
Which of these characteristics do you feel you need the most improvement in and why?

HOMEWORK

Mentoring

In early recovery I learned the value that mentors can provide in terms of advocating for an individual's needs, navigating complex systems like school or legal, and problem-solving challenges as they occur. As I began working towards completing my education, a mentor became incredibly important for supporting my goals. They worked with me to establish SMART, incremental goals focusing on aspirations that were aligned with my personal strengths.

Having someone to process setbacks and career accomplishments with kept me engaged in my recovery process of cultivating self-worth and potential for growth. Each week my mentor played an instrumental role in helping me build self-efficacy by role modeling effective communication skills and study habits. Through principled, trauma informed discussions, I gained insight on managing emotions, navigating past traumas that once felt paralyzing, and maintaining overall Wellness using skills like time management.

How Does the Passage connect to Mentoring or Resonate with You?

HOMEWORK

Question– 1:
What is a SMART goal? What is 1 SMART goal related to your strengths that will improve your life? How will this goal improve your life?

HOMEWORK

Question– 2:

How does gaining insight into your strengths create the possibility to aid others? How could being of service to others keep you engaged in the recovery process?

HOMEWORK

Question– 3:

Has anyone ever acted as a role model who offered to teach you effective study skills? What did they suggest to help study better? Out of all the advice you may have been given about study skills, what would you recommend to another person as being the most helpful tool?

HOMEWORK

The Homework – In the next Year I will

For the current year;

- Create a Recovery Plan Involving 7 goals/activities that you have every day and some activities you will need to do every once in awhile. In the area for the date, if it is not ongoing, list the date of completion; if it is ongoing, state whether it is something that is done every day, or how often it will be done. Please include **both** daily tasks and those we must do every now and then.

- Start with things you struggle with rather than things you find easy.

- Next, create a list of 7 big goals you have, or things that are vitally important that you want to or must do within the year.

- Ensure that this list/Recovery Plan includes how you will support your basic needs like shelter, food and bills. Make the goal specific and attainable.

- During Day 4 we will present a goal from each category of the Recovery Plan and the action steps for the goal.

NOTES:

Radical Recovery Peer Support - University Day 3

Honesty

Many of us have Baggage. In recovery, we may resist new healthy behaviors and thoughts. This may often stem from a lack of honesty about three factors, 1: that we have been hurt, 2: that we have hurt ourselves or others, and 3: the nature of the severity of the hurt.

It is important to acknowledge

- if we are not honest with ourselves about how we have been hurt, hurt ourselves or others, or the severity, we may repeat unfavorable experiences.

- Lets take a minute to be honest with ourselves about ourselves. On page 149 and 150 you will find a list of virtues, values, and character defects. Please read the directions and complete the activity. Every person has some of each, please indicate at least <u>five</u> of each.

Honesty

Honesty was one of the hardest recovery concepts for me to embrace early on. For so long, I had hidden from the truth about ways I had been hurt and had hurt others through my own actions. Living with so many secrets and a distorted view of reality kept me stuck in unhealthy behaviors. When I first started participating in a peer support group, I was afraid to be truthful about my experiences and struggles. I didn't want others to judge me or for my secrets to be revealed.

It wasn't until I opened up to a mentor that I really began making progress. They showed me unconditional support and helped me understand the importance of being honest with myself first. With their guidance I gradually started sharing more of my story with others in the group. Each time I did, I felt a weight being lifted off my shoulders. I realized I wasn't alone in my experiences and others weren't judging me like I feared.

Being honest helped me gain clarity and acceptance of my past. It opened the door to recovery concepts like hope, responsibility, and trust, that allowed me to start moving in a positive direction. Now, honesty is the foundation that keeps me grounded in my recovery. My life has changed for the better because of embracing this important concept.

How Does the Passage Connect to Honesty or Resonate with You?

HOMEWORK

Question - 1:
How easy or difficult do you find it to be honest with yourself about ways you have been hurt by others or have hurt others through your own actions? What is one experience that has led you to feel this way?

HOMEWORK

Question - 2:
When sharing aspects of your experiences and struggles with others, how do you balance being honest while also feeling comfortable?

HOMEWORK

Question - 3:
What could you do to build your level of trust in others so that honest disclosure feels less risky? Give an example of something that might be good not to talk about with people you're not sure you can trust, and give an example of something that is usually OK to share with others that will not lead to consequences?

HOMEWORK

1. -

2. -

3. -

Honesty

I did not perform well academically in the past due to various life challenges. I questioned whether I was even capable of succeeding in school. However, I realized I needed to be honest with myself that my past struggles did not define my potential and it was these struggles (not necessarily a lack of effort) which had held me back from my education.

In college, I committed to putting in genuine effort through honest and ethical work. I understood the importance of academic integrity as dishonesty would only hinder my learning and preparation for future careers. While the course work was difficult at times and there were many temptations to shortcut my responsibilities, maintaining honesty helped me persevere. I focused on studying diligently and completing all assignments to the best of my ability.

Through practicing honesty, I gained self-respect and built trust within myself that I could achieve my academic goals through earnest participation. My professors also recognized my commitment, which boosted my confidence further. Looking back now, I see how developing integrity set strong foundations for my continued education and career path. It has allowed me to take pride in my accomplishments rather than living with regret. Overall honesty has been an empowering part of my recovery.

How Does the Passage Connect to Honesty or Resonate with You?

HOMEWORK

Question - 1:

How can being honest with yourself about your past academic struggles help you overcome feelings of self-doubt about your potential for success in any kind of school?

HOMEWORK

Question - 2:

In what ways can maintaining honesty help you persevere when life or coursework get difficult?

HOMEWORK

Question - 3:

How can practicing honesty build self-respect and trust within yourself in your ability to achieve your academic and career goals?

HOMEWORK

NOTES:

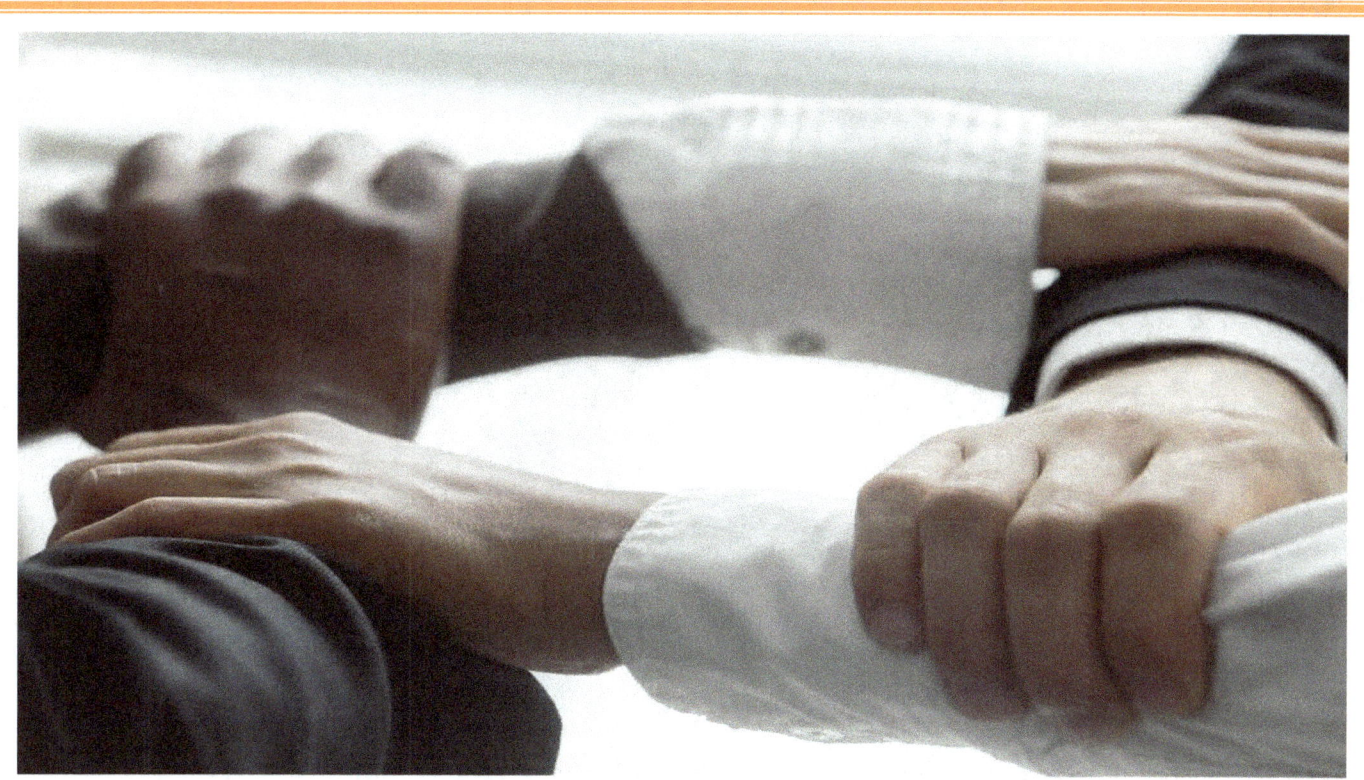

Trust

There are different levels of trust:

We can have trust in

- a specific person or people that we trust
- in the systems we are in, such as our governments, legal system, or system of wellness or therapy
- self-trust; <u>trusting that we have our own best interests in mind</u>.

Within these is determining who we can rely on, who we cannot, and what we can share with others.

Tip – (Trust)

❖ **Self-disclosure: It is important to remember**
- we never need to share something that would make us uncomfortable
- there is more we can share with others than something that would make us uncomfortable
- it is different to share things we want to keep private versus our hopes, goals, and stresses
- there is no guarantee what we say will remain confidential

Trust

When I first considered pursuing my education after years of struggle, I didn't know if I could trust that higher education would be worth the significant costs and efforts involved. I questioned whether college was just another "system" trying to control people for its own profit motives.

However, as I observed others who had faced similar challenges as me succeed through higher education, it gave me reason to believe the "system" could not be built entirely on lies or empty promises. While teachers in colleges are not perfect, focusing on my own dedication and persistence helped overcome potential frustrations with my inability to trust in a brighter future.

I also had to trust that each educational experience, such as assignments and courses, would teach me valuable skills and take me closer to achieving my goal. Practicing trust was not always easy as my attention was constantly divided between school and fulfilling other responsibilities like my recovery, family, and work.

The difficulty of school is a natural "hurdle," but hard work is what gives education its value and separates achievers from non-achievers. Learning to accept uncertainties and have faith in my own abilities allowed me to persevere despite doubts about higher education. In the end, taking that initial leap of trust empowered my recovery journey and allowed me to graduate as a lower-level honors student!

How Does the Passage Connect to Trust or Resonate with You?

HOMEWORK

Question - 1:
Do you feel like college or technical school is built on a lie or is a trap to get you to owe someone money or that it is something that can provide a valuable experience?

HOMEWORK

Question - 2:
Do you trust that college or technical school will be worth the cost and effort?

HOMEWORK

Question - 3:
How can learning to accept uncertainties and having trust in your ability help you persevere when you are in doubt?

HOMEWORK

Trust

For me, trust was an issue that took a long time to develop, both with myself and others on my journey to recovery and higher education. In my past, I experienced a great deal of conflict and struggle, with not knowing who I could trust and who would offer me genuine and helpful support. This relates directly to the concept of trust.

Having safe, trustworthy people to lean on is so important to recovery from addiction or mental health issues. Feeling less alone and having others who understand my struggle makes the path forward much more achievable, and college is a wonderful place to find many unique and different people to connect with.

When I first entered higher education, I did not believe I could truly succeed after years of past failures. But through surrounding myself with a support network of peers, mentors, academics and recovery community members, I was able to start building trust that has been so meaningful in my ongoing recovery and academic journey. These people helped me believe in myself.

Being able to be vulnerable, to ask for help when I needed it, and to open up to others in a supportive community has created countless opportunities to further develop trust within myself and with others.

How Does the Passage Connect to Trust or Resonate with You?

HOMEWORK

Question - 1:

How have past experiences of conflict and struggle led you to have difficulty trusting others to offer genuine and helpful support?

HOMEWORK

Question - 2:

In what ways can surrounding yourself with a support network of peers, mentors, academics and recovery community members help you start building trust in yourself and your ability to succeed?

HOMEWORK

Question - 3:

How can having companionship and someone to trust help support your ongoing recovery and academic journey?

HOMEWORK

NOTES:

Acceptance

Each person is subject to different degrees of unforeseen circumstances, restrictions, rules, and regulations. For the most part, these obstacles depend on our situation, can be temporary, or can be changed with support. While we must deal with these situations while they occur, we can find ways to have hope within them and have Better Days.

*Tip – Trauma/Grief Informed: Many people will report that there are things that they cannot or will not accept. This is okay, remind them that they can still work on other Fundamentals and that there is a difference between 1: accepting that an event took place and 2: accepting an event into our lives and our space.

WE MUST KEEP MOVING

Sometimes, it is the things we find the hardest to accept that take us off the path of our life purpose.

Dr. Martin Luther King Jr. believed that the most important thing each person must do is figure out their life purpose and let nothing hold them back from being the very best at the purpose they have chosen.

While we may struggle to find acceptance, we can let nothing hold us back; in the words of Dr. King **"We must keep moving. If you can't fly, run; if you can't run, walk; if you can't walk, crawl; but by all means keep moving."**

Acceptance

Before I returned to college, I was so hard on myself for the past mistakes and difficulties I faced in high school. It took accepting where I was at and focusing on growing from that point for things to really start improving.

In classes, there were times I struggled with course material or managing my workload alongside outside responsibilities. It was easy to feel ashamed about that and to feel like I wouldn't be able to do it. But once I accepted that setbacks and imperfect progress were normal parts of the process, I could focus on doing my best without that extra burden of harsh self-criticism. That made it easier to ask for help from professors or peers when needed.

On a larger level, gaining acceptance of my situation and myself allowed me to fully commit to my education by acknowledging and making peace with my past and present limitations. I had so much more mental and emotional energy to dedicate to my studies. I didn't have to spend time wishing things were different or beating myself up for where I started. I could own my reality while still striving to grow through my college experience. I think acceptance was an invaluable component of bettering my situation.

How Does the Passage Connect to Acceptance or Resonate with You?

HOMEWORK

Question - 1:
What past mistake or difficulty do you most struggle to accept?

HOMEWORK

Question - 2:
How can accepting your limitations allow you the opportunity to create problem solving solutions that will help you strive to grow?

HOMEWORK

Question - 3:
How can acceptance help you move forward in a healthy way and commit more fully to your goals?

HOMEWORK

Acceptance

Throughout my bachelor's degree I found myself frequently feeling discouraged by unforeseen challenges and circumstances that seemed too difficult to overcome. As someone maintaining recovery from substance use and mental health while pursuing an education, any new stressors or obstacles felt like threats that could jeopardize all the progress I had made.

There were certainly times when my responsibilities outside of school, from legal troubles to marital issues, made dedicating time and energy to my studies feel nearly impossible. It was so easy to believe those problems meant putting my education on hold or even giving up on that goal entirely. In fact, I did give up after my first year of college which was almost eight years before I began my recovery journey and finally returned to finish my degree.

However, through acceptance I found another path. By acknowledging the reality of my situation without judgment, I could stop viewing setbacks as signs of failure. Coming to terms with current situations allowed me to problem solve constructively instead of emotionally reacting in all or nothing terms. I discovered valuable support systems within recovery groups and communities that help shoulder burdens through difficult patches and reduced my courseload when I felt I needed a break.

How Does the Passage Connect to Acceptance or Resonate with You?

HOMEWORK

Question - 1:
What is one recent unexpected challenge or situation that has threatened your progress?

HOMEWORK

Question - 2:
What is your perception of this challenging situation? How could viewing the setback or challenge from question #1 as a sign of failure, rather than accepting it and moving forward, impact your ability to create a solution that will help you continue to grow?

HOMEWORK

Question - 3:

Sometimes we find our life situations unacceptable. Maybe these situations further our purpose or goals, or maybe they do not. If your current situation provides for your basic needs but you find yourself feeling it's not the best situation for you, how can you accept it for what it is and pursue change?

HOMEWORK

Accepting Your Life – (Page 42)
Original Peer Support Recovery & Coping Skills Workbook and Curriculum

Life happens.

Life will go on whether things have been fair or not.

Life will go on if you have made a big mistake.

Life will go on if you win $1,000,000.

Life will go on no matter what.

Life will go on if you break your arm.

Life will go on if you have surgery.

Life will go on if you have a financial crisis.

I life will go on. Your life will continue.

Accepting Your Life (Continued)

We must accept that life will happen and sometimes there is nothing that we can do about it. If we suffer pain, loneliness, regret, embarrassment or any other difficult feeling, we must accept our life. We must accept our life and we must accept our reality. We must also accept that each and everyone of us has the power within to make a Better Day for ourselves no matter what the circumstances we find ourselves in.

Life will go on no matter what.

I know that I will live my life fighting for that Better Day because I have to.

I have no other option. Better Days are on the way and Better Days are here to stay.

How Does the Passage Connect to Acceptance or Resonate with You?

HOMEWORK

Question - 1:
What are three things that you feel are unfair about your life?

HOMEWORK

1. -

2. -

3. -

Question - 2:
In what three ways do you live your life in a hopeful way?

HOMEWORK

1. -

2. -

3. -

Question - 3:
What are three steps that you could take to make your life better today?

HOMEWORK

1. -

2. -

3. -

Day 4 - Introduction

Please be prepared to discuss a goal for each category of your 1-year Recovery Plan.

Have a great week!

NOTES:

Hope

If we are struggling to find hope, it will often become easier the longer we commit to recovery and with more time between distressing events. Also, we can seek out inspiration by:

- talking to supporters about what is giving our supporters hope
- making lists of things that give us hope
- reading recovery stories
- listing our dreams, and if possible, communicating them to someone

Hope – (Page 4)
Original Peer Support Recovery & Coping Skills Workbook & Curriculum

On Somedays, hope is all I have.

I will fight to live a better life because I want to be happy and successful and because I deserve it.

No one else can tell me that I can't have a better life in which I am happy and healthy.

We decide if we want to live a good and healthy life.

We must reject negative and unhelpful thinking.

Each of us has the power within us to change for the better.

Each of us has a responsibility to work as hard as we can to improve our lives.

We are in control of our lives. Allow yourself to be in control of your life.

We will rise above stigma and be all that we can be.

It will be your victory.

How Does the Passage Connect to Hope or Resonate with You?

HOMEWORK

Question - 1:
What are five things that I am proud of in my life?

HOMEWORK

Question - 2:
What are five things that I most want to improve in my life?

HOMEWORK

Question - 3: Recovery is -?

HOMEWORK

Hope

As someone in recovery pursuing higher education, I can speak to the importance of hope from my own experiences. When I was younger, living with untreated mental health and substance use issues, I had very little hope for my future. I believed the negative impressions others had of me and felt incapable of achieving my dreams.

Pursuing higher education was a big goal that first seemed unattainable. Research shows that people with hope tend to have greater success in school. For me, developing hope was so important because it helped me trust that completing my education could actually lead to positive change, even when the process was difficult. Every assignment I finished and every class I passed brought me closer to receiving my degree. Seeing others with similar experiences graduate gave me evidence that investing in higher education could pay off.

While the education system is not perfect, having hope allowed me to believe it was not built on a lie intended to control people and make money. That hope, developed through the help of others and small successes along the way, provided the motivation I needed to persevere in my recovery journey and academic career. I am grateful that rekindling my hope has opened so many doors to a brighter future.

How Does the Passage Connect to Hope or Resonate with You?

HOMEWORK

Question - 1:
How has the negative criticism of others and/or self-doubt impacted your belief in your ability to develop or achieve goals?

HOMEWORK

Question - 2:
What are two small successes you've had recently or witness others achieving that helped provide motivation for your recovery?

HOMEWORK

Question - 3:

In what ways does developing hope combat feelings that education is not worth investing in or that it's "built on a lie"?

HOMEWORK

Hope

It took a few years of being in recovery for me to get rid of most of my self-doubt, which I had a lot of when I started. Growing up I didn't have many positive role models who believed in me or encouraged me to pursue my dreams and goals. I struggled with this self-doubt and didn't think I was capable of much.

It wasn't until I met a peer supporter during treatment that my perspective on hope began to change. They were one of the first people who genuinely believed I had potential and could accomplish things if I set my mind to it. We had many conversations where they asked me what I wanted for my future and encouraged me to start small with achievable goals.

I slowly realized that by achieving small goals and tasks I could build my skills over time. That gave me hope that one day I could pursue bigger dreams like getting a college degree. Going back to school seemed impossible when I was deep in addiction but taking it step by step helped hope grow in my heart. I started with getting sober then working on life skills. Each step forward strengthens my belief that I could keep going.

How Does the Passage Connect to Hope or Resonate with You?

HOMEWORK

Question - 1:
How could feedback and guidance from a positive role model impact your belief in your ability to achieve your goals?

HOMEWORK

Question - 2:

How does achieving small goals and tasks help provide motivation to pursue larger dreams like higher education by building skills and hope overtime?

HOMEWORK

Question - 3:

In what ways has accomplishing the initial phases of your recovery strengthened your ability to believe in yourself to continue making progress?

HOMEWORK

NOTES:

Personal Responsibility

Some situations may be out of our control or cause discomfort for us. If we are having a hard time fulfilling responsibilities because of obstacles, things outside our control, or things we need or are worried about; we can ask how much control we have over these situations, and if we are doing everything we can within the control we have.

To get back on track we can follow a Recovery Plan that involves:

- A daily plan
- A plan of things we need to do every now and then
- A plan for achieving big goals

Plans should include a way to provide for ourselves and elements of Self-Care.

Personal Responsibility (Continued)

If we are developing a Recovery Plan, it is important to first list things we struggle with, things that need the most attention, or that create new responsibilities for us.

A Recovery Plan is a way to familiarize ourselves with our objectives and requirements and decide how things need to be done.

Personal Responsibility may involve creating goals that improve our lives and our success. For information on how to help someone with their goals, refer to the section of the RRPS Recovery & Mentorship Guide titled Motivational Interviewing & Recovery Planning.

Personal Responsibility

Before I began my recovery, I used to think that I was perfect, and that all problems were because of other people or situations that were outside of my control. I believed that I lacked resources and opportunity because that's just what my situation was. I missed work frequently and thought that it was OK because I had my own worries to deal with. I was struggling, and that was my excuse.

I had no concept of personal responsibility when I began recovery. It's easy to blame outside obstacles for difficulties fulfilling responsibilities. In the early days of my recovery, I made so many excuses about why I wasn't succeeding. I spent more time engaging in unhelpful activities and behaviors instead of studying. It took some challenges and setbacks for me to realize that no matter what outside factors are present I do have control over how I choose to spend my time.

Once I started treating my education like a job and made academics the priority is when I really began to make progress. I took advantage of campus resources like tutoring and office hours when I needed extra help and I showed up to every class on time and prepared. While perfection wasn't realistic, simply completing all of my assignments to the best of my ability helped me demonstrate personal responsibility.

How Does the Passage Connect to Personal Responsibility or Resonate with You?

HOMEWORK

Question - 1:
Before beginning recovery, how much control did you believe you had over problems and difficulties in your life?

HOMEWORK

Question - 2:
How much control do you believe you have today?

HOMEWORK

Question - 3:
How do you usually spend your time, can you afford to make changes to prioritize your education?

HOMEWORK

Personal Responsibility

Struggling with mental health and addiction, I was used to blaming others for my shortcomings and character defects. Going back to college required me to take accountability for my own actions and make a commitment to my education. I found that small changes to my lifestyle dramatically improved my success. It wasn't enough to passively go through the motions, I needed to be an active participant in my education.

At first, having that level of responsibility was challenging and I struggled with time management, would miss deadlines, and wasn't using resources like tutoring as much as I needed. It was an adjustment to treat my education as something I was fully in charge of rather than something being done to me. This was also my choice, which was empowering because I hadn't had the freedom to make many choices of my own before starting college.

Personal responsibility has been a big part of my recovery journey. Seeing that I was capable of managing my academic responsibilities and achieving my goals helped shift my mindset from one of a victim to one of having agency and control over my own life. It taught me that with commitment to doing the work, I had the ability to succeed. This translates beyond school and carries over to taking responsibility for my overall wellness and recovery. Personal responsibility is an important recovery principle that I continue working on every day.

How Does the Passage Connect to Personal Responsibility or Resonate with You?

HOMEWORK

Question - 1:

Do you have any challenges or shortcomings that would be easy to fix? List 3 and give an example of how you can take accountability for improving the outcome.

HOMEWORK

1-

2-

3-

Question - 2:

If you have been in recovery for a little while, how has taking responsibility changed your perspective on your life? Do you have a better or worse image of yourself than when you started the recovery process?

HOMEWORK

Question - 3:

Can you translate small successes with taking responsibility into success in higher education, such as taking one class at a time, doing 3 hours of homework per week, or easily accessing and watching a video about how to write good papers? Can you write a list of your interests and then pursue them?

HOMEWORK

Personal Responsibility

After many difficult years of struggling with addiction and mental health issues, I hit my rock bottom. It was around that time that I started to take recovery more seriously and decided I wanted to make a change. I realized that in order to truly recover I needed to start taking responsibility for improving my life and future. One of the first steps I took was enrolling in college.

At first, I struggled with time management, motivation, and consistency, but I slowly started making progress by setting small achievable goals for myself like not drinking or getting high while studying or doing homework, completing assignments by their due dates, and earning at least a passing grade.

By this point, personal responsibility has become very important in my Day-to-day life. Staying on top of my schoolwork, budgeting my time carefully and overcoming challenges help me feel empowered and in control of my life. For me going to college was all about making a goal for myself that would improve my life and my success.

How Does the Passage Connect to Personal Responsibility or Resonate with You?

HOMEWORK

Question– 1:
What are the biggest challenges you believe you will face in school or getting into school?

HOMEWORK

Question– 2:
In what ways can you address the challenges from question #1 that will show you have been responsible in searching for opportunity?

HOMEWORK

Question– 3:
Is there anyone you can talk to who can tell you about different careers, locations of the nearest schools, requirements for being admitted, or help you prepare skill wise or in general for college? Find the name of one such professional and write their number in the space below.

HOMEWORK

Question– 4:
How much time can you begin to commit per day or per week to learn a new skill?

HOMEWORK

NOTES:

Self-Advocacy – (Page 12)
Original Peer Support Recovery & Coping Skills Workbook & Curriculum

Throughout much of my life, I can remember that I have had many times that I needed someone to help me and speak up on my behalf. I had so many needs that were not addressed. Even to this day, I am aware of the extreme damage that has been done to me after years of not having my needs met. As a teenager growing up in many unnatural situations, no one spoke up and advocated for my personal and intimate needs. I was just another troubled teenager living in a group home.

One thing that I wish I learned as many years ago was the act of self-advocacy. After living through some extremely dreadful and horrendous situations, I have learned how to better advocate for myself. Most everything that I have in my life, I have as a result of my self-advocacy.

When we are able to effectively speak up about our needs, then our lives will be better. Self advocacy is our tool - Use it!

Self-Advocacy

Sometimes people may feel they have lost their right or ability to advocate for themselves, or that they have lost control of their lives. Each person has the right to advocate for themselves for public benefits and treatment common to their society no matter what the state of their lives.

*Tip – if a person is having a hard time gaining support through self-advocacy, communicate that

- our chances of getting support increase the longer we maintain continued effort with the Recovery Fundamentals that precede this step, especially Personal Responsibility.

- we can believe in ourselves and practice advocating by making a list of goals we think will get the most support and advocating for each item on the list.

What Mentors Should Know

- System Level Advocacy – Advocating for changes to rules, policies, or laws that affect how someone lives their lives.

- Self Adovcacy – Because very few people will advocate for us, and because recovery is person-driven, self-advocacy, the process of explaining why you deserve or are qualified for something, is the foundation for a strong recovery.

- Shared decision making – This is the process of a supporter and the person being supported collaborating to develop action plans that are agreed to by both partys.

- Person centered language – Instead of saying "he is an addict", say "name* is a person with an addiction. Instead of saying "they are Bipolar", say "name* is a person diagnosed with Bipolar." Instead of saying "they are a patient", say "name* is a person who is receiving services." Instead of saying "Bro", "Dude", or "Man", say "name*."

What Mentors Should Know

Navigating Services - Mentors will regularly require the services of other professionals to provide support and often make recommendations and referrals for other services. A mentor makes meaningful connections with many local services and leaders. Knowing when to say we don't have all the answers is an important characteristic of a mentor. Finding other providers of services who understand the significance of recovery and wellness versus treatment, and the specific needs for people facing specific challenges is encouraged.

Advocating for Recovery-Oriented Systems involves knowing the organization and leaders of the systems in your area on a deep level. We should develop close relationships with people who might provide recovery services to the people we serve. These deep relationships will inform us if the provider has a recovery-oriented mindset for which to advocate. A Recovery Oriented System of Care is a network of community-based services that meet the total needs of the person in recovery or their families. This includes emotional, occupational, educational, financial, spiritual, physical health, social, and environmental needs.

How Does the Passage Connect to Self-advocacy or Resonate with You?

HOMEWORK

Question– 1:
Give one example of a time in which you advocated for your needs.

HOMEWORK

Question – 2:
What is one example where you did not speak up in order to have your needs met and what would you do differently next time?

HOMEWORK

Question – 3:
What do the words "self-advocacy" mean to you?

HOMEWORK

Self-advocacy

Growing up I was used to having my requests and thoughts ignored. It was like everything I said was falling on deaf ears. I was often told that I was to be seen and not heard and that children didn't deserve respect, so I became uncomfortable speaking up about what I needed. This neglect instilled a pattern in me and enforced the belief that no one would listen so why bother saying anything. I kept so much bottled up that I felt like I was going to explode.

When I entered recovery and started working on myself, the importance of self-advocacy really began to click for me. I realized that in order to succeed I couldn't just hope things would work out on their own I needed to take charge of my life and ask for help when I needed it. After this when I hit roadblocks in my classes, instead of giving up easily, I made appointments with my professors and tutors. I explained how my disability impacted my learning and asked for accommodations like no time limits on tests. This was approved by my college.

It was really empowering to see that when I advocated for myself, people were willing to work with me. With some small adjustments, I was able to thrive where before I would have struggled silently. Self-advocacy has definitely been a key in my recovery journey and education.

How Does the Passage Connect to Self-advocacy or Resonate with You?

HOMEWORK

Question – 1:
How do you usually communicate your needs, strengths, and skills? Give an example of how you have communicated a need, a strength, or a skill.

HOMEWORK

Question – 2:
Give an example of a strength and give an example of a skill. Can this strength and this skill help you as a student or in your job? How can you advocate to others about this strength or skill?

HOMEWORK

Question– 3:
What is one job or career that your strength and your skill would be a benefit for?

HOMEWORK

Self-advocacy

My experience with self-advocacy in college set me up well for the future. As I got closer to graduating, I began applying for jobs, I knew I couldn't keep my talents and skills a secret like I once had. In order to show potential employers all that I was capable of I had to speak up confidently about my strength's, qualifications, and work style.

I made sure to emphasize how I could contribute as an employee, and because of my willingness to self-advocate, I secured a few good positions even though I had a criminal record. I realized that if I wanted to succeed, advocating for myself could no longer be optional. It was a key part of my recovery journey and professional success.

How Does the Passage Connect to Self-advocacy or Resonate with You?

HOMEWORK

Question– 1:
Before beginning your recovery journey or even currently how did or do difficulties and barriers in your life shape your view on speaking up about your needs.

HOMEWORK

Question – 2:
Do you believe you have strengths and skills that would be of value to others?

HOMEWORK

Question – 3:
What is your most unique positive characteristic? Describe a situation where you have used this to benefit yourself or others.

HOMEWORK

Day 5 Introduction

- Please be prepared to share one goal from each category of your 3-year Recovery Plan for the next group.

NOTES:

Day 5

Support

"It takes support to fulfill BIG goals. If we do not look for support or accept support from the right people, we will have a tougher time achieving our goals."

If we lack support, developing a strong support system benefits from:

- being mutually supportive to others
- doing everything within our control to maintain our personal definition of wellness
- becoming active in the community, a support group, school or other area like employment
- having several supporters so someone will always be available, and we do not overburden anyone.

Dealing With Conflict: Trusting Others – (Page 34)
Original Peer Support Recovery & Coping Skills Workbook and Curriculum

In my life, I have experienced a great deal of conflict. At times, I have struggled with knowing which people I can get the most helpful support from. This is an issue of trust. Let's talk about what trust is and how having a trustworthy confidant is important to your recovery: having a safe person who you can trust to help you is important. Having that person will help you feel less alone in your struggle.

As people in recovery, our lives present countless opportunities for us to develop trust in others and to learn to trust ourselves. We can create better days, one trusting moment at a time because we do not need to be alone in our struggle.

How Does the Passage Connect to Support or Resonate with You?

HOMEWORK

Question– 1:
List the names of three people who you can trust if you are having an intense challenge.

HOMEWORK

Question– 2:
How do you manage a tough situation when you don't have someone to talk to for support?

HOMEWORK

Question– 3:
Why is being able to trust others important to your recovery?

HOMEWORK

Support

While my journey through higher education wasn't exactly straightforward, I found support through honest self-examination and from others in recovery. When I first started college, I was skeptical it could truly help someone like me. As someone in long term recovery I had doubts that the system would accept me for who I was. Over time, I realized the importance of being honest about my experiences and trusting that others had good intentions.

Most helpful were conversations with my advisors and mentors in the recovery community. They encouraged me to be upfront about my struggles so I could get the right accommodations and not feel alone. Opening up about my past wasn't easy but it allowed others to understand where I was coming from. I also discovered many others currently in college who shared similar experiences.

Realizing we all deal with struggles of some kind helped me accept myself. It became clear that with effort and honesty about what support I needed, higher education could still be within reach. These days I try to do the same for others in recovery thinking of going back to school. With support from both the academic and recovery communities, any of us can work to improve our situation through education.

How Does the Passage Connect to Support or Resonate with You?

HOMEWORK

Question– 1:

Do you believe there is adequate support for your educational and career needs and interests?

HOMEWORK

Question– 2:

What support options interest you the most? Choices might include getting a mentor, seeing a tutor, turning your writing in to an online writing coach, taking advantage of an instructor's office hours, or speaking with the disability office at your school.

HOMEWORK

Question– 3:

Have you identified any other people that have a similar background to you that you might be able to receive support from and offer support to?

HOMEWORK

NOTES:

Purpose

Once we have maintained progress relevant to our interests and security, are more empowered, and have support, we may find that other people are an extension of ourselves or that we have integrated a cause into our lives.

We may also find that
- human rights
- dignity

and
- freedom

become important to us.

Life Blueprint– Purpose
Dr. Martin Luther King Jr.

"You're going to be deciding as the days and the years unfold, what you will do in life, what your life's work will be.

Once you discover what it will be, set out to do it and do it well.

Be a bush if you can't be a tree.

If you can't be a highway, just be a trail.

If you can't be the sun, be a star, for it isn't by size that you win or you fail, be the best of whatever you are."

Purpose

When I first began my recovery journey, I did not have a clear sense of purpose. I struggled to see what meaningful activities or career paths were available to me. However, as I engaged in my education and explored different interests, I started to gain clarity. While in school, I was able to experience various opportunities to help me discover where my passions truly lie.

Although I initially felt my chosen purpose would take a long time to achieve or that I lacked the ability, continuing my education provided hope. I found that my interest did change and evolve over time as I gained new knowledge and experiences. Things that once seemed too complex became clearer as I learned more.

Looking back through notes and journals, I was able to see my own personal growth. While I may not have mastered every aspect of my desired field by graduation, I had made significant progress in finding my purpose. My education played a key role in my recovery by providing direction, motivation, and a sense of accomplishment. It has helped me to reclaim something lost from my past and work towards a stable future through a meaningful career. Overall, my purpose continues to drive me forward in both my recovery journey and higher education.

How Does the Passage Connect to Purpose or Resonate with You?

HOMEWORK

Question– 1:

Even if you have very little interest in anything, what is the industry, job, career or field that is the most interesting to you at this point in time? What is something small you can do to find out more information?

HOMEWORK

Question– 2:

How might accomplishing smaller instrumental goals help inspire you and boost your self-esteem and confidence as you work towards your longer-term goals?

HOMEWORK

Question– 3:
How can continuing to educate yourself and learn help drive yourself discovery process, even if you have not yet found your definitive purpose?

HOMEWORK

Purpose

Looking back on my recovery journey, I think one of the most inspiring things I experienced that helped me was finding my purpose, an extremely important Recovery Fundamental. Even though I was in college in recovery it took years for me to discover my purpose. I struggled to find meaning and motivation. However, as I engaged in school and I explored different career options through coursework and extracurricular activities, I started gaining clarity on what I was passionate about.

Developing instrumental goals helped me work towards discovering my purpose. These were smaller, action-oriented objectives I could focus on in the short term to make progress on larger, long term aims. For example, one of my instrumental goals was to gain experience in different fields related to my interests through internships or volunteering which allowed me to test out career paths in a low-pressure environment and receive feedback.

Another goal was to build relevant technical skills through hands on learning opportunities like certifications. Accomplishing these instrumental goals helped boost my self-esteem and confidence in pursuing my chosen field, helping me to find purpose and feel confident. Higher education gave me hope that even if I did not immediately find my purpose, I would evolve as I learned which further drives the self-discovery process.

How Does the Passage Connect to Purpose or Resonate with You?

HOMEWORK

Question– 1:
Have you found that developing goals for yourself and making progress relevant to your security and interests empowers you and provides hope? What is one goal you have set for yourself before you started this program?

HOMEWORK

Question– 2:
What is one thing you could do to help your community or someone in it? The first thing that comes to mind might be a purpose you can pursue.

HOMEWORK

Question– 3:
When life presents extra stresses, to whom do you turn for support to keep you motivated and moving forward?

HOMEWORK

Purpose

In my early recovery, I felt unsure about what I was interested in and how I could turn those interests into a meaningful career. My focus was on improving my personal well-being and security through recovery activities like attending support groups, counseling, and practicing self-care. As I worked on my mental health, stability, and bad habits, I started to feel ready to explore other opportunities.

I began connecting more with my peers through school and volunteering. These social interactions helped me gain perspective on my abilities and what I enjoyed.

It was through making progress in my personal development and feeling more secure that I was empowered to learn about different career paths. I started to see higher education as a way to turn my interests into a purpose. Classes provided knowledge that helped me determine if certain fields were a good fit. I also found mentors, both professional and peers, who gave guidance that further supported my path of self-discovery.

How Does the Passage Connect to Purpose or Resonate with You?

HOMEWORK

Question– 1:
What do you think it takes to turn your interests into a meaningful career? Give an example of one interest that under the best circumstances and with unlimited resources you think you could turn into a career or business.

HOMEWORK

Question– 2:
What are the support groups, therapies, or volunteering experiences that you have been involved with that have helped you gain the most perspective on your abilities and interests? Could participating in these areas turn into a purpose for you?

HOMEWORK

Question– 3:

Many people often find purpose in the things that bring them closer to their communities, how could higher education be a way for you to become more connected with the community around you? Would being connected with hard working and considerate people that have vision be something you would look forward to?

HOMEWORK

NOTES:

Self-Actualization

Self-actualization is all about reaching the true potential of our unique selves. Once we have reached our full potential, we may find that we are freer and more capable.

People at this level of development may begin to have a deeper connection with where they believe they fit in the universe, existence, in relation to other people, or with their concept of a higher power.

Self-Actualization (continued)

In the Allegory of the Cave from Plato's *The Republic*, the principal character in the story returns to people who were still "disillusioned" to help them find a better way.

For many, there is a natural inclination by this stage of recovery, to show others a brighter future.

The Parallel Recovery Concept of Mentorship has carried many individuals' recoveries to particularly new heights. Consider the shift in growth demonstrated in the Linear Growth Model due to the Recovery Concept of Mentorship.

Living the Life You Want to Live – (Page 48)
Better Days A Mental Health Recovery Workbook

Before 2006, I had never heard of the concept of recovery. I had no idea that people living with mental health issues could get better and live decent lives. I always had so many dreams, goals and aspirations that, unfortunately, had not become reality. This was and is something that is very frustrating for me, and I would imagine that I am not the only person who can relate to this. In order to lead the life I want to live, I need to consider that my dreams and goals are real possibilities so that I can work toward living a happier life day, by Better Day, by a Better Day, by Better Day.

With hard work and dedication, you can lead a happier, healthier and more satisfying life.

How Does the Passage Connect to Self-Actualization or Resonate with You?

HOMEWORK

Question– 1:
What are three goals that you have in your life?

HOMEWORK

Question– 3:
What are two steps that you could take to help yourself achieve your goals?

HOMEWORK

Self-actualization

Self-actualization is not just something that we work for and never achieve, it is a destination that we can arrive at and remain at throughout the rest of our lives. Before I began recovery, I didn't have much sense of who I truly was or what I was capable of. Years of coping with mental health and substance use issues chipped away at my self-esteem and self-worth. Pursuing education gave me goals to work toward that helped increase my self-efficacy.

As I succeeded in my courses despite challenges, it helped me realize how resilient I was and how many talents and strengths I possessed. Succeeding in higher education made me feel like I was starting to uncover my true potential and live in a way that was fulfilling to me.

Education has also supported my recovery by providing me with a structure and purpose each day. Staying engaged and learning has meant that I have been less likely to revert to old coping habits. I also found that as I continue to learn and better myself, it has nourished my soul in a way that improved my mental well-being.

Overall working towards personal growth and self-actualization through higher education align well with the core recovery principle of living a self-directed life because it creates new choices for us. While my journey is still ongoing, and I haven't exactly reached that final destination, I now believe in myself and know I will get there someday. I also know from seeing the success of others, that the effort will truly be worth it for me.

How Does the Passage Connect to Self-Actualization or Resonate with You?

HOMEWORK

HOMEWORK

Question– 1:
In what ways did unhealthy influences and coping mechanisms convince you that you are limited in what you could achieve? How has succeeding in early recovery no matter how small the success given shape to a better life today?

Question– 2:
What role does persevering while gaining new skills and knowledge play in cultivating self-efficacy and finding passion?

Question– 3:
Name a person whose life you have seen improve as a result of education, and write down what they are doing now.

HOMEWORK

NOTES:

Recap & Conclusion

This curriculum emphasizes balanced linear growth through the development of 9 Recovery Fundamentals and three Parallel Recovery Concepts that occur alongside each of the 9 Fundamentals.

 **The goals of this program are based on the Fundamentals of Recovery and the Recovery Concepts and are to teach participants how to:**

 Learn to develop a Recovery Plan to take recovery to greater heights (Recovery Planning)

 Learn the importance of and how to perform Self-Care

 overcome challenges or troubling thoughts, handle stressful or difficult situations, achieve personal growth and wellness, and live a self-directed life

 learn that while participating in recovery we are at every moment a mentor and a model of recovery behavior

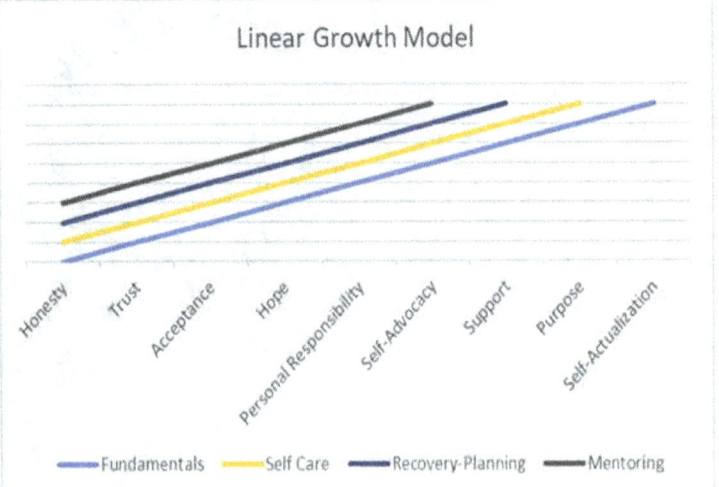

The Linear Growth Model

The Linear Growth Model gets its name from the idea that

- Growth is usually Non-Linear

- we want to put consistent effort into each of the 9 Fundamentals which will result in more, but not all, consistent experiences in our lives.

- When developed inconsistently with this format, inconsistent and unexpected outcomes may occur.

- When developed in the order listed previously, each of the 9 Recovery Fundamentals assists in the cultivation and growth of the other Fundamentals.

- When Utilizing the Parallel Recovery Concepts in conjunction with the Recovery Fundamentals, we can shift our results to a better outcome

Mahatma Gandhi, the great Indian spiritual leader, said, "Be the change you want to see in the world."

From the Better Days workbook passage *Creating Change*: "I say that first I must change myself into the person I want to be."

The words from the passage *Creating Change* and Mahatma Gandhi indicate that by learning to focus on our personal experience of growth and change in the direction of our own interest, the world, will change in our direction, as we model the behaviors we want to see in the world.

Many programs say that giving back and helping others with the same problems as we have experienced is a sort of final step. Many people who have been successful in Recovery say that **giving back, taking commitments to support others,** and **remembering that they are an example of recovery in their communities** helped them the most in their recovery.

The reasoning of this program and in Peer Support in general is that showing recovery is possible occurs alongside every stage in the process and our actions create a lasting impact.

Stages of Wellness and Recovery:

Stage one
1- Learning about recovery
2- Exercising choice
3- Seeking services i.e. counseling, therapy, medication, detox, peer support
4- Staying away from harmful behaviors
5- Staying away from negative influences, places or people
6- Ending the pattern of isolation
7- Finding positive role models
8- Learning to ask for support
9- Becoming personally responsible
10- Experiencing joy and distress that can be overwhelming at times (extreme but fickle)

Stage 2
1- Increase in physical health
2- Ability to distinguish between different feelings and handle them
3- Reducing emotions that interfere with our wellbeing
4- Changes in thoughts, feelings and beliefs
5- Zoning in on negative behaviors
6- Having experienced the benefits of recovery, becoming committed to recovery

Stage 4
1- Ability to use our strengths & knowledge to seize opportunities
2- Automatic use of wellness tools and coping skills
3- Self-forgiveness
4- Building loving relationships rather than dependent ones
5- Experiencing enduring happiness

Stage 3
1- Desire to make amends for harm we caused before we began recovery
2- Becoming the "change we want to see in the world"
3- Learning not to inflict self-harm or create hardship
4- Developing honest and trusting relationships with more people

Stage 5
1- Becoming Self-actualized
2- Gaining confidence, gratitude, and acceptance
3- Developing integrity and humility
4- Significant reduction of fear

Stage 6 - Celebration & Maintenance

The 10 Guiding Principles of Recovery

Taken From SAMHSA

Hope – belief that recovery is possible. When Hope is internalized and promoted by others, it is a key driver of recovery.

Person-driven – People define their own goals and the path to reaching them. Noone achieves them for us.

Many Pathways/Roads – Recovery is highly personalized and different for each person.

Holistic – Recovery emphasizes mind, body, spirit, and community.

Peer Support – Peers encourage and engage each other.

Relational – Recovery is supported by people who believe in a person's ability to recover.

Culture – Traditions, beliefs, and values are important in defining a person's recovery journey and path.

Trauma-informed – Support should promote safety and trust, creating choice, empowerment, and collaboration.

Strengths & Responsibilities – Individuals, communities, and families have strengths and resources that can benefit recovery. Individuals have the responsibility for their own recovery, but family and community support are essential.

Respect – acceptance and appreciation are key to recovery. This includes respect from other people and a respect for ourselves that help us develop a positive identity and confidence.

What Mentors Should Do

- Identify personal issues that negatively impact one's ability to perform mentor duties and perform appropriate self care before assisting others further.
- Utilize consultation regarding dual relationships.
- Utilize de-escalation techniques and educate individuals on suicide prevention concepts.
- Partner with the individual to access recovery-oriented services and supports
- Support the individual to identify options and participate in decisions connected to creating and completing recovery goals.
- Promote a wellness-focused approach to recovery.
- Utilize supervision and consultation regarding harm to self and others.
- Respond appropriately to personal stressors, triggers and indicators.
- Utilize trauma-informed care approaches.
- Assess the mentee's satisfaction with his/her progress toward recovery goals.

What Mentors Should Know

- System Level Advocacy – Advocating for changes to rules, policies, or laws that affect how someone lives their lives.
- Self Adovcacy – Because very few people will advocate for us, and because recovery is person-driven, self-advocacy, the process of explaining why you deserve or are qualified for something, is the foundation for a strong recovery.
- Shared decision making – This is the process of a supporter and the person being supported collaborating to develop action plans that are agreed to by both partys.
- Person centered language – Instead of saying "he is an addict", say "name* is a person with an addiction. Instead of saying "they are Bipolar", say "name* is a person diagnosed with Bipolar." Instead of saying "they are a patient", say "name* is a person who is receiving services." Instead of saying "Bro", "Dude", or "Man", say "name*."

What Mentors Should Do

- Participate as a member of the individual's treatment team.
- Guarantee that recovery is based on the individual's strengths and resiliencies.
- Support the individual in defining spirituality on their own terms.
- Assist others to develop problem-solving skills.
- Assure that relationships, services and supports, reflect individual differences and cultural diversity.
- Support the individual's use of self-determination.
- Model acceptance and cultural humility.
- Partner with individuals to assist them in identifying their strengths, challenges to recovery and recovery capital.
- Apply Motivational Interviewing to assist individuals in during stages of change.
- Inform individuals of their options related to decisions that affect their recovery.

What Mentors Should Know

Navigating Services - Mentors will regularly require the services of other professionals to provide support and often make recommendations and referrals for other services. A mentor makes meaningful connections with many local services and leaders. Knowing when to say we don't have all the answers is an important characteristic of a mentor. Finding other providers of services who understand the significance of recovery and wellness versus treatment, and the specific needs for people facing specific challenges is encouraged.

Advocating for Recovery-Oriented Systems involves knowing the organization and leaders of the systems in your area on a deep level. We should develop close relationships with people who might provide recovery services to the people we serve. These deep relationships will inform us if the provider has a recovery-oriented mindset for which to advocate. A Recovery Oriented System of Care is a network of community-based services that meet the total needs of the person in recovery or their families. This includes emotional, occupational, educational, financial, spiritual, physical health, social, and environmental needs.

VIRTUES & VALUES

Please circle each value you feel describes who you are. Reflect on if you hold these values in high regard and what it means to you to posses this value. Consider if the values you didn't circle are important to you and determine what it would look like for you to posses that value and how you can incorporate it into your lifestyle. <u>Try to be as honest with yourself as you can during this exercise.</u> This is not an extensive list.

Orderliness	Generosity	Courage	Wisdom
Justice	Self-control	Assertiveness	Helpfulness
Modesty	Peacefulness	Service	Forgiveness
Purposefulness	Good Counsel	Responsibility	
Kindness	Honesty	Respect	Tolerance
Perseverance	Good judgment	Gratitude	Humility
Obedience	Patience	Leadership/Command	
Truthfulness	Moderation	Loyalty	Courtesy
Friendliness	Sincerity	Prayerfulness	
Greatness/Magnanimity		Docility	Industriousness
Foresight	Patriotism		
Meekness	Tact		

CHARACTER DEFECTS

Please circle each character defect you feel describes who you are. Reflect on your thoughts about the defects you circled. Determine if you would like to make a change to improve in these areas. <u>Try to be as honest with yourself as you can during this exercise.</u> This is not an extensive list.

Resentment	Cowardice	Self-Pity
Self-Justification	Self-Importance	Self-Condemnation
Lying and Evasiveness	Impatience	Hate
False Pride	Jealousy	Envy
Laziness	Procrastination	Insincerity
Negative Thinking	Immoral Thinking	Perfectionism
Criticizing	Greed	Distrustfulness
Hypochondria	Being Thin-Skinned	Moodiness
Being a Buzzkill	Willful Ignorance	callousness
Cruelty	Violence	Rigidity
Diffidence	Lechery	Self-Indulgence
Being a Know-It-All	Naiveté	Immaturity
Fastidiousness	Being overly picky	Prejudice
Rudeness	Crassness	

Note: You can use the pages with lines to add extra action steps that can't be fit into the colored tables.

"What I do in the 168 hours of the week."
Be as specific as possible, have at least 1 activity for every line, you can do multiple activities at the same time.

_____

_____

_____

_____

_____

_____

_____

_____

_____

_____

_____

Year 1 – Everyday Goals

Goal #1 _____

_____

Strengths & Recovery Capital	Obstacles	Action Steps	Date of Completion

Goal #1
Goal Description
_____

Action Steps

- _____
  _____
  _____

- _____
  _____
  _____

- _____
  _____
  _____

- _____
  _____
  _____

- _____
  _____
  _____

- People

  Involved_____
  _____

- _____
  _____

Year 1 – Everyday Goals

Goal #2 _____

_____

Strengths & Recovery Capital	Obstacles	Action Steps	Date of Completion

Goal #2
Goal Description
_____

Action Steps

- _____
  _____

- _____
  _____
  _____

- _____
  _____

- _____
  _____

- _____
  _____

- People

  Involved_____

  _____

- _____

  _____

Year 1 – Everyday Goals

Goal #3 _____

_____

Strengths & Recovery Capital	Obstacles	Action Steps	Date of Completion

Goal #3
Goal Description
_____

Action Steps

- _____
  _____

- _____
  _____

- _____
  _____

- _____
  _____

- _____
  _____

- People

  Involved_____
  _____

- _____
  _____

Year 1 – Everyday Goals

Goal #4 _____

_____

Strengths & Recovery Capital	Obstacles	Action Steps	Date of Completion

Goal #4
Goal Description
_____

Action Steps

- _____

   _____

- _____

   _____

- _____

   _____

- _____

   _____

- _____

   _____

- People

   Involved_____

   _____

- _____

   _____

Year 1 – Goals We Need Once in a While

Goal #5 _____

_____

Strengths & Recovery Capital	Obstacles	Action Steps	Date of Completion

Goal #5
Goal Description
_____

Action Steps

- _____
  _____
  _____

- _____
  _____
  _____

- _____
  _____
  _____

- _____
  _____
  _____

- _____
  _____

- People

  Involved_____
  _____

- _____
  _____

Year 1 – Goals We Need Once in a While

Goal #6 _____

_____

Strengths & Recovery Capital	Obstacles	Action Steps	Date of Completion

Goal #6
Goal Description
_____

Action Steps

- _____
  _____
  _____

- _____
  _____
  _____

- _____
  _____
  _____

- _____
  _____
  _____

- _____
  _____

- People

  Involved_____

  _____

- _____

  _____

Year 1 – Goals We Need Once in a While

Goal #7 _____

_____

Strengths & Recovery Capital	Obstacles	Action Steps	Date of Completion

Goal #7
Goal Description
_____

Action Steps

- _____

 _____

- _____

 _____

- _____

 _____

- _____

 _____

- _____

 _____

- People

 Involved_____

 _____

- _____

 _____

Year 1 – Big Achievements

Goal #8 _____

_____

Strengths & Recovery Capital	Obstacles	Action Steps	Date of Completion

Goal #8
Goal Description
_____

Action Steps

- _____
 _____
 _____

- _____
 _____
 _____

- _____
 _____
 _____

- _____
 _____
 _____

- _____
 _____
 _____

- People Involved_____
 _____

- _____
 _____

Year 1 – Big Achievements

Goal #9 _____

_____

Strengths & Recovery Capital	Obstacles	Action Steps	Date of Completion

Goal #9
Goal Description
_____

Action Steps

- _____
  _____
  _____

- _____
  _____
  _____

- _____
  _____
  _____

- _____
  _____
  _____

- _____
  _____
  _____

- People

  Involved_____

  _____

- _____

  _____

Year 1 – Big Achievements

Goal #10

_____

_____

Strengths & Recovery Capital	Obstacles	Action Steps	Date of Completion

Goal #10
Goal Description
_____

Action Steps

- _____
  _____
  _____

- _____
  _____
  _____

- _____
  _____
  _____

- _____
  _____
  _____

- _____
  _____
  _____

- People Involved_____
  _____

- _____
  _____

Year 1 – Big Achievements

Goal #11

_____

_____

Strengths & Recovery Capital	Obstacles	Action Steps	Date of Completion

Goal #11
Goal Description
_____

Action Steps

- _____
  _____

- _____
  _____
  _____

- _____
  _____
  _____

- _____
  _____
  _____

- _____
  _____

- People

  Involved_____
  _____

- _____
  _____

Year 1 – Big Achievements

Goal #12

_____

_____

Strengths & Recovery Capital	Obstacles	Action Steps	Date of Completion

Goal #12
Goal Description
_____

Action Steps

- _____
  _____

- _____
  _____
  _____

- _____
  _____

- _____
  _____

- _____
  _____

- People

  Involved_____
  _____

- _____
  _____

Year 1 – Big Achievements

Goal #13
_____

_____

Strengths & Recovery Capital	Obstacles	Action Steps	Date of Completion

Goal #13
Goal Description
_____

Action Steps

- _____

  _____

- _____

  _____

- _____

  _____

- _____

  _____

- _____

  _____

- People

  Involved_____

  _____

- _____

  _____

Year 1 – Big Achievements

Goal #14

_____

_____

Strengths & Recovery Capital	Obstacles	Action Steps	Date of Completion

Goal #14
Goal Description
_____

Action Steps

- _____
  _____

- _____
  _____
  _____

- _____
  _____
  _____

- _____
  _____

- _____
  _____

- People
  Involved_____
  _____

- _____
  _____

Note: You can use the pages with lines to add extra action steps that can't be fit into the colored tables.

3 year – Everyday Goals

Goal #1 _____

_____

Strengths & Recovery Capital	Obstacles	Action Steps	Date of Completion

Goal #1
Goal Description
_____

Action Steps

- _____
  _____

- _____
  _____

- _____
  _____

- _____
  _____

- _____
  _____

- People
  Involved_____
  _____

- _____
  _____

3 year– Everyday Goals

Goal #2 _____

_____

Strengths & Recovery Capital	Obstacles	Action Steps	Date of Completion

Goal #2
Goal Description
_____

Action Steps

- _____
  _____

- _____
  _____
  _____

- _____
  _____

- _____
  _____

- _____
  _____

- People
  Involved_____
  _____

- _____
  _____

3 year– Everyday Goals

Goal #3 _____

_____

Strengths & Recovery Capital	Obstacles	Action Steps	Date of Completion

Goal #3
Goal Description
_____

Action Steps

- _____
  _____

- _____
  _____

- _____
  _____

- _____
  _____

- _____
  _____

- People
  Involved_____
  _____

- _____
  _____

3 year– Everyday Goals

Goal #4 _____

_____

Strengths & Recovery Capital	Obstacles	Action Steps	Date of Completion

Goal #4
Goal Description
_____

Action Steps

- _____
  _____
  _____

- _____
  _____
  _____

- _____
  _____
  _____

- _____
  _____

- _____
  _____

- People

  Involved_____
  _____

- _____
  _____

3 year– Goals We Need Once in a While

Goal #5 _____

_____

Strengths & Recovery Capital	Obstacles	Action Steps	Date of Completion

Goal #5
Goal Description
_____

Action Steps

- _____
  _____
  _____

- _____
  _____
  _____

- _____
  _____
  _____

- _____
  _____
  _____

- _____
  _____
  _____

- People
  Involved_____
  _____

- _____
  _____

3 year– Goals We Need Once in a While

Goal #6 _____

_____

Strengths & Recovery Capital	Obstacles	Action Steps	Date of Completion

Goal #6
Goal Description
_____

Action Steps

- _____

    _____

- _____

    _____

    _____

- _____

    _____

- _____

    _____

- _____

    _____

- People

    Involved_____

    _____

- _____

    _____

3 year– Goals We Need Once in a While

Goal #7 _____

_____

Strengths & Recovery Capital	Obstacles	Action Steps	Date of Completion

Goal #7
Goal Description
_____

Action Steps

- _____

 _____

- _____

 _____

- _____

 _____

- _____

 _____

- _____

 _____

- People

 Involved_____

 _____

- _____

 _____

3 year – Big Achievements

Goal #8 _____

_____

Strengths & Recovery Capital	Obstacles	Action Steps	Date of Completion

Goal #8
Goal Description
_____

Action Steps

- _____
  _____
  _____

- _____
  _____
  _____
  _____

- _____
  _____
  _____

- _____
  _____
  _____

- _____
  _____
  _____

- People

  Involved_____

  _____

- _____

  _____

3 year– Big Achievements

Goal #9 _____

_____

Strengths & Recovery Capital	Obstacles	Action Steps	Date of Completion

Goal #9
Goal Description
_____

Action Steps

- _____
  _____
  _____

- _____
  _____
  _____

- _____
  _____
  _____

- _____
  _____
  _____

- _____
  _____
  _____

- People

  Involved_____

  _____

- _____

  _____

3 year– Big Achievements

Goal #10

_____

_____

Strengths & Recovery Capital	Obstacles	Action Steps	Date of Completion

Goal #10
Goal Description
_____

Action Steps

- _____
  _____

- _____
  _____
  _____

- _____
  _____

- _____
  _____

- _____
  _____

- People

  Involved_____
  _____

- _____
  _____

3 year – Big Achievements

Goal #11

_____

_____

Strengths & Recovery Capital	Obstacles	Action Steps	Date of Completion

Goal #11
Goal Description
_____

Action Steps

- _____

  _____

- _____

  _____

  _____

- _____

  _____

  _____

- _____

  _____

- _____

  _____

- People

  Involved_____

  _____

- _____

  _____

3 year– Big Achievements

Goal #12

_____

_____

Strengths & Recovery Capital	Obstacles	Action Steps	Date of Completion

Goal #12
Goal Description
_____

Action Steps

- _____
  _____
  _____

- _____
  _____
  _____

- _____
  _____
  _____

- _____
  _____
  _____

- _____
  _____

- People

  Involved_____
  _____

- _____
  _____

3 year– Big Achievements

Goal #13

_____

_____

Strengths & Recovery Capital	Obstacles	Action Steps	Date of Completion

Goal #13
Goal Description
_____

Action Steps

- _____

  _____

- _____

  _____

- _____

  _____

- _____

  _____

- _____

  _____

- People

  Involved_____

  _____

- _____

  _____

3 year– Big Achievements

Goal #14

_____

_____

Strengths & Recovery Capital	Obstacles	Action Steps	Date of Completion

Goal #14
Goal Description
_____

Action Steps

- _____
  _____
  _____

- _____
  _____
  _____
  _____

- _____
  _____
  _____

- _____
  _____
  _____

- _____
  _____

- People

  Involved_____
  _____

- _____
  _____

10 Year – Everyday Goals

Goal #1 _____

_____

Strengths & Recovery Capital	Challenges	Action Steps	Date of Completion

Goal #1
Goal Description
_____

Action Steps

- _____
  _____
  _____

- _____
  _____
  _____

- _____
  _____
  _____

- _____
  _____
  _____

- _____
  _____

- People
  Involved_____
  _____

- _____
  _____

10 Year – Everyday Goals

Goal #2 _____

_____

Strengths & Recovery Capital	Challenges	Action Steps	Date of Completion

Goal #2
Goal Description
_____

Action Steps

- _____
  _____
  _____

- _____
  _____
  _____

- _____
  _____

- _____
  _____

- _____
  _____

- People Involved_____
  _____

- _____
  _____

10 Year– Everyday Goals

Goal #3 _____

_____

Strengths & Recovery Capital	Challenges	Action Steps	Date of Completion

Goal #3
Goal Description
_____

Action Steps

- _____
  _____
  _____

- _____
  _____
  _____

- _____
  _____
  _____

- _____
  _____
  _____

- _____
  _____
  _____

- People

  Involved_____
  _____

- _____
  _____

10 Year– Everyday Goals

Goal #4 _____

_____

Strengths & Recovery Capital	Challenges	Action Steps	Date of Completion

Goal #4
Goal Description
_____

Action Steps

- _____
  _____

- _____
  _____
  _____

- _____
  _____

- _____
  _____

- _____
  _____

- People

  Involved_____

  _____

- _____
  _____

10 Year– Goals We Need Once in a While

Goal #5 _____

_____

Strengths & Recovery Capital	Challenges	Action Steps	Date of Completion

Goal #5
Goal Description
_____

Action Steps

- _____

  _____

- _____

  _____

  _____

- _____

  _____

- _____

  _____

- _____

  _____

- People

  Involved_____

  _____

- _____

  _____

10 Year – Goals We Need Once in a While

Goal #6 _____

_____

Strengths & Recovery Capital	Challenges	Action Steps	Date of Completion

Goal #6
Goal Description
_____

Action Steps

- _____
  _____

- _____
  _____
  _____

- _____
  _____

- _____
  _____

- _____
  _____

- People
  Involved_____
  _____

- _____
  _____

10 Year – Goals We Need Once in a While

Goal #7 _____

_____

Strengths & Recovery Capital	Challenges	Action Steps	Date of Completion

Goal #7
Goal Description
_____

Action Steps

- _____
  _____

- _____
  _____
  _____

- _____
  _____

- _____
  _____

- _____
  _____

- People
  Involved_____
  _____

- _____
  _____

10 Year – Big Achievements

Goal #8 _____

_____

Strengths & Recovery Capital	Challenges	Action Steps	Date of Completion

Goal #8
Goal Description
_____

Action Steps

- _____
  _____

- _____
  _____

- _____
  _____

- _____
  _____

- _____
  _____

- People Involved _____
  _____

- _____
  _____

10 Year – Big Achievements

Goal #9 _____

_____

Strengths & Recovery Capital	Challenges	Action Steps	Date of Completion

Goal #9
Goal Description
_____

Action Steps

- _____
  _____
  _____

- _____
  _____
  _____

- _____
  _____
  _____

- _____
  _____
  _____

- _____
  _____
  _____

- People

  Involved_____

  _____

- _____
  _____

10 Year – Big Achievements

Goal #10

_____

_____

Strengths & Recovery Capital	Challenges	Action Steps	Date of Completion

Goal #10
Goal Description
_____

Action Steps

- _____
  _____

- _____
  _____

- _____
  _____

- _____
  _____

- _____
  _____

- People

  Involved_____
  _____

- _____
  _____

10 Year – Big Achievements

Goal #11

_____

_____

Strengths & Recovery Capital	Challenges	Action Steps	Date of Completion

Goal #11
Goal Description
_____

Action Steps

- _____

   _____

- _____

   _____

   _____

- _____

   _____

- _____

   _____

- _____

   _____

- People

   Involved_____

   _____

- _____

   _____

10 Year – Big Achievements

Goal #12
_____

_____

Strengths & Recovery Capital	Challenges	Action Steps	Date of Completion

Goal #12
Goal Description
_____

Action Steps

- _____

  _____

- _____

  _____

  _____

- _____

  _____

- _____

  _____

- _____

  _____

- People

  Involved_____

  _____

- _____

  _____

10 Year – Big Achievements

Goal #13

_____

_____

Strengths & Recovery Capital	Challenges	Action Steps	Date of Completion

Goal #13
Goal Description
_____

Action Steps

- _____
  _____

- _____
  _____

- _____
  _____

- _____
  _____

- _____
  _____

- People

  Involved_____
  _____

- _____
  _____

10 Year – Big Achievements

Goal #14

_____

_____

Strengths & Recovery Capital	Challenges	Action Steps	Date of Completion

Goal #14
Goal Description
_____

Action Steps

- _____
  _____

- _____
  _____

- _____
  _____

- _____
  _____

- _____
  _____

- People

  Involved_____
  _____

- _____
  _____

Facilitation Process

Level 1 Groups – Co-facilitator Required*

The slides that can be read in the workbook or PowerPoint will be divided between all those wishing to receive a certificate of participation or completion, including participation from the facilitators. The Facilitators will start by explaining why we request full participation and the reward of either a certificate of completion or participation. The Information on participation requirements is on page two underneath the table of contents.

The Facilitators will read the first two slides of the first presentation. After that, all slides will be divided up between the participants. The exceptions to this are the slides in the first session's presentation following the slide title "Why We Present the Recovery Fundamentals and Parallel Recovery Concepts in this Order." These slides sometimes contain more than one Fundamental or Concept and there will be a different reader for each of these.

At the end of each session, the Facilitator will read the last slide that conveys information related to the upcoming session. After this, the remainder of the time will be spent on open discussion of the day's session. For session one this will be the full span of 2 hours, for the remaining session it will be the span of 3 hours.

The remaining sessions also have sections titled 'How does this passage connect or relate to the concept or fundamental.' These questions entail a short response that should connect the passage read just before this question to the Recovery Concept or Fundamental being discussed at the time. Everyone has the capability to answer these questions so everyone desiring a certificate of participation or completion will answer these including the facilitator, unless facilitator participation means some participants will not have the chance to participate.

Participation points will not be lost for these questions if there were not enough questions for everyone to get a chance to participate. A participation sheet will be provided which specifies how many participation points a person will need in each category of participation. For those who have not had a chance to answer these questions, they will have an opportunity to revisit them at the end of the group.

Sessions 2 – 5 also have many short questions. There are usually 3 questions for each passage. These are divided between all those seeking a certificate of completion and the Facilitators. These questions are not required to be answered by those seeking a certificate of participation.

The Facilitator will not participate or read unless there are fewer than 5 people attempting a certificate of completion, in which case, only participating when they have the least amount of participation compared to those seeking a certificate. Participants can choose when they would like to participate in order to get the right amount of participation points, however when some of them are close to full points, the facilitator will begin asking specific people to participate if a participant has the least amount of participation.

If participants do not have a response to a particular question, the Facilitator will step in and answer the question. If participants did not get enough participation points from this question-and-answer section, we can allow them to answer other questions from the session at the end as a revisitation.

To revisit a question requires them to have completed enough of their answers to share them and receive the required completion points. This might be useful for participants that did not complete enough of their questions before the group where the questions they did answer in the book were answered by other participants. Even if the participant did not complete a question before group, we can allow them to develop a quick answer on the spot if they are able.

Once the presentation process is over for the session, we allow the rest of the time to be open discussion starting with the facilitator asking the group if they have any questions, allowing participants to ask questions here. Next, we will do a check in, asking the group how they are doing with the concepts or fundamentals covered in the session. Once 2 hours have elapsed for session one, or three hours for all other sessions, the session is complete.

This is how the group will be Facilitated.

Continuum Groups – Level 2 Group

The continuum groups are meant for people who have already participated in a regular group and who have a desire to participate in a longer-term group. Also, in cases where a Facilitator does not have a Co-facilitator, they can provide Continuum Groups instead. If a Co-facilitator is available, we should always try to do the level 1 group first so that people who want either of the two certificates can get them and they can receive a reward or token from the group in the form of a certificate of participation (not of completion) or a coin (coins which we will make soon.) Level 2 groups will also provide a certificate or coin, however only after 52 sessions have been completed.

In this type of group, the Facilitator does not need to discuss participation requirements. Also, the first session will be given out as a packet of paper to any participants attending the group for the first time. By doing this, we skip session 1 and actually present material starting with session 2.

Sessions 2-5 will be broken down into 3 groups apiece. Instead of presenting all of the material for session 2, we will present the material for the concepts of Self-care, Recovery Planning, and Mentorship on three different days. We will separate the fundamentals from sessions 3-5 in the same way, tackling them in three days rather than in one.

The participants do not need to bring their books or read any slides. In this version of the group, the Facilitator reads everything. There is the introduction material starting with each concept or fundamental, followed by an inspirational passage, followed by asking the question "How does this passage relate to the 'concept' or 'fundamental.'

In asking this question, in the level 1 group, we like everyone to have already answered this question in their books and to read their response for the group. In this case, we ask them to answer the question spontaneously with the thoughts they have at the moment. This should ensure that even if they answer the question similarly each time, they may have noticed a connection today different from what they wrote in their books or answered in a previous level 2 group.

After this question, there are generally 3 questions asked that relate to the passage or recovery in general. These questions will also be answered spontaneously without the use of their book. These questions are usually something that they have experienced in more than one way and can provide different answers to each time they come across them.

Level 2 groups are meant to be an hour long. If the group runs shorter than this period, facilitators can do a check-in, asking how participants are experiencing the concept or fundamental in their lives. This group is meant to be continuous, thus the word Continuum in the name. While we will present the material in 12 weeks, people may want to continue them longer because with new participants being added consistently there should be diversity in how people answer questions over time.

This is how the group should be operated.

How to Become an RRPS Facilitator

To become an RRPS Facilitator, you must first, participate in an RRPS group. You cannot become a Facilitator for each of the different groups by only participating in one type of group. In order to qualify as a Facilitator of a specific group, a potential Facilitator has to participate in that specific group.

There are three different programs or groups. Radical Recovery Peer Support (RRPS), RRPS-University, and RRPS-Liberation. RRPS is for people who are experiencing general distress. RRPS-University is for people experiencing distress but who are either attempting a form of education beyond k-12, or who are thinking about doing so. RRPS-Liberation is for people with a criminal history that includes Driving Under the Influence.

At the present time, RRPS liberation training is only for potential Facilitators who have a criminal record or whose criminal records were expunged or pardoned. In the future, anyone can become an RRPS-Liberation Facilitator if they know another RRPS-Liberation facilitator, believe that the program is helping people with criminal records, and receive a written recommendation from an RRPS-Liberation Facilitator stating they believe you have the ability to work well with participants of this background or that they can attest that you have worked with this group of people before.

For RRPS-University, a Facilitator must show proof that they have at least 25 credits of college experience, or that they have received a certification in a particular skill and have worked in that field for 3 years.

For the RRPS program specifically, other than RRPS-University or RRPS-Liberation, there are no background requirements to become a Facilitator.

*After personally participating in a group, the Facilitation training will begin. Facilitation training involves working with an Advanced Level Co-Facilitator to present a group to 3 people (no more than 3). They will do this on a recorded Zoom session so the recording can be viewed to make sure the presentation process went smoothly. The low number of participants will ensure that the facilitator will also participate, as participation is divided among the participants and the Facilitators when the number of people attempting a certificate of completion is less than 5 persons.

For more information on how to divide the participation during a regular (non-training group) consult the text on page two of the Facilitator handbook. Or check out our blog titled "Participation Requirements" at www.communitypeerservices.com/blog This blog also states the amount of completion of the workbook needed by each person attempting to become a Facilitator.

During training, the potential Facilitator is not required to examine participants workbooks for completeness, this will be for their Advanced Level Co-facilitator to complete.

A potential Facilitator may need to find participants for their training group. We cannot guarantee that we will have willing participants. This means a Facilitator in training must find three people who want to get certified. We suggest trying to network with others in the mental health recovery, substance use recovery, or criminal Reentry fields such as Peer Supporters, or Forensic Peer Supporters via your social media.

The fee for participation in a group is $187.50 and the fee for the training opportunity is also $187.5. Payment plans are available upon request but for a higher overall price of $250.00 divided among 52 weeks. Anyone who does not pay their payment plans on time will have their certifications suspended. This means that they will not be able to provide certificates of completion that will be accepted by us, which means that the people participating in a group with a Facilitator who has been suspended will not be able to become facilitators and will need to do the group with a facilitator who is current with their payments.

Once a person participates in a Facilitator training program, they are qualified to Facilitate any group without having to run a practice group for each (as long as background requirements are met). However, they will need to earn a certificate of completion for each group they want to Facilitate.

Author's note:

Hi, I am Dakota Fisher.

I designed this group because I believe in recovery. This will probably not be the only tool in your recovery toolbox, because a toolbox that has only one tool in it usually doesn't have much value. I hope that people participating in this program develop a system of recovery that works for them.

There are many systems of recovery that I participate in because my mind needs continual education concerning the issues I face. With respect to educating myself on these issues, I know that 1000 programs might never be enough to relieve me of an insanity that had at one time completely overtaken my ability to function productively and happily in society and my community.

My beliefs, thoughts, and feelings became twisted in a way that I could not see anything of value in the world and had become hopeless. No tool that I discovered had a complete answer because all of them were made by people who have different and unique views on recovery and had different experiences that helped them become thoughtful in specific areas.

Because no one has an exact recipe for how to help you recover, as only you can discover the mix of thoughts, beliefs, and feelings that work for you, it might be hard to find what is needed to begin and complete your recovery journey. In the worst instances, some of the people or programs we reach out to for help will try to convince us that their program is the best and that we should pick one above the others and commit to it.

From my perspective, one of the most important things in my recovery was not the programs themselves, but the people I would meet in a program that would become part of my support group. Having these people in my life helps me stay open-minded; moreover, it ensures that I usually have someone in recovery around me at all times, and if not, they are only a phone call away.

The way I see it, I need a diverse group of supporters, because each person in my circle only knows the part of the picture that they have experienced or been exposed to. A lot of times, people who are very knowledgeable about one thing do not have any valid answers to certain problems I have experienced. So, if one person doesn't have an answer, I need to find someone who does. This can only be accomplished by meeting them where they are at, wherever they are at.

In some cases, I will find that I can't entirely agree with a particular philosophy, or that a person who is supposed to be providing me with aid does not understand where I am coming from or why I feel the way I feel. I might sometimes be considering finding a new supporter. When this happens, I do not curse the whole program or field of care because of my bad experience. Most of the resources out there provide value to many people, or else they would not survive.

Therefore, it is important for me to carefully consider what it is about a program or person that I am in disagreement with and see if there is another option that will provide me with the best benefits that that program, service, or person offers. This might require a searching and fearless education into recovery resources to find out about their purpose, and their promises.

If I feel like something is not to my liking or is adversely affecting me, I want to have supporters, or trusted friends or family members who I can ask if they have noticed unpleasant changes or if they think I've been doing better. Sometimes it is hard for me to tell because I have had many intermingling problems that clouded my judgement. Having these people around will allow us to bring them to our appointments and explain what they are seeing in such cases where we want a change to be made but the person we are relying on to make the change doesn't listen to us or believe we are seeing clearly.

So, this program and education are both tools we might want in our toolbox. Other important "tools" or "resources" are having an open mind and having a willingness to experience new things. Open-mindedness and willingness will allow us to take advantage of the good aspects of any program and leave behind what doesn't work for us.

As a final note, one of the most pervasive and underlying concepts of this program is mentorship. The difference between mentorship and sponsorship is not so evident at first glance, but there are some distinguishing features. Sponsors of certain programs are indeed meant to practice the principles they have learned in all areas of their lives, but most people in this position will not be sponsors at work, school, or public places. They reserve their sponsorship for people with the particular issues that underlie their program of choice. A sponsor will usually not discuss issues that are outside of their primary area of concern. Some sponsors will say ambiguously that if we refrain from harmful behaviors everything will fall into place.

A Mentor will be a mentor in all places and for any issue. Mentors exhibit the best version of themselves in the work they do, in their field of study, in social and recreational settings, etc... Because we never know where we will meet a person that needs our help, we will try to live to our fullest potential so that when a person asks us how we handle situations with such grace, or where we find our motivation, we can tell them. Living our fullest potential will attract people to our way of life. Mentors will also be willing to talk about any facet of life with a person who is struggling even if they are not the best resource for that particular concern and will try to connect the person to someone with more insights if they find they cannot offer meaningful aid. We are always mentors, and our behavior will influence people for good or bad whether we know it does or not.

Authors Background

*United States Army Veteran

*BS Finance (honors)

*Current MBA student

*Pennsylvania - Certified Peer Specialist

*Forensic Peer Specialist

*MRT Facilitator

*Mental Health First Aider

**Formerly Incarcerated Person

References

- King, M. L., Jr. (1967, October 26). What Is Your Life's Blueprint? Barratt Junior High School in Philadelphia, Pennsylvania.

- King Jr., M. L. (1965, March 25). Keep Moving from This Mountain [Speech]. Spelman College, Atlanta, Georgia.

Prison Partnership Program (PPP)

Our goal is to have our group available at every prison in America. We can't do this without your help. If you work at a prison, visit our website www.communitypeerservices.com and click "contact" to reach out and find out how to become a Facilitator of our group.

Our intention is for the inmates themselves to work as Peer Supports in the prison and facilitate the groups themselves. However, we would need a staff member to oversee the group process to make sure the group is conducted appropriately.

IF YOUR CURRENTLY SERVING TIME IN PRISON – If your facility does not offer this group, we have a correspondence course available where you can earn a certificate that might help you be approved for parole. The more you work on your wellness, the better chance you have of reducing your sentence. Write to Community and Peer Services at 1016 Memorial Avenue, Williamsport, PA, 17701 to find out how to get involved in the program. Pass this along to others who might want to benefit from this opportunity who might not have heard of the program.

Radical Recovery Peer Support University

Community & Peer Services
Caps

Community & Peer Services
Caps

Community & Peer Services
Caps

To Explore Our Website go to

www.communitypeerservices.com

To learn more about our different group or training programs visit
www.communitypeerservices.com/blog

Find us on:
Facebook @ Community and Peer Services
LinkedIn @ Community and Peer Services
Twitter @2023caps
Reddit @ #RadicalRecovery
YouTube @ #RadicalRecovery

www.ingramcontent.com/pod-product-compliance
Lightning Source LLC
Chambersburg PA
CBHW081615100526
44590CB00021B/3447